Decimus et Ultimus Barziza, Representative from
Harris County, 1875. Taken from an individual
photograph of Barziza as a member of the Fifteenth
Legislature, House of Representatives, the Capitol,
Austin, Texas.

Decimus et Ultimus Barziza

THE ADVENTURES
OF A PRISONER
OF WAR
1863–1864

Edited by R. Henderson Shuffler

UNIVERSITY OF TEXAS PRESS, AUSTIN

To
Samuel Paul Houston,
William Alexander Anderson (Bigfoot) Wallace,
and innumerable other sons
of the Old Dominion, who,
like Decimus et Ultimus Barziza,
added a cavalier touch to the Texas tradition.
From them alone could we have inherited
that inordinate pride in place of origin
which distinguishes Texans—and Virginians—
from ordinary folk.

PREFACE

The Adventures of a Prisoner of War; and Life and Scenes in Federal Prisons: Johnson's Island, Fort Delaware, and Point Lookout; by An Escaped Prisoner of Hood's Texas Brigade has long been one of the rarest and least known of the published memoirs of Texans who fought in the Civil War. Until recently only one copy, held in the Archives Division of the Texas State Library, was available to the general public. There it was catalogued only under the name of the publishers. A photostatic copy of the book was in the Texas Collection at the Barker History Center of The University of Texas, where it had been identified as the work of D. U. Barziza by the late Dr. E. W. Winkler.

This is the only known published memoir of a Texan who wrote of his experiences as a prisoner during the Civil War and one of the few such accounts published on either side before the end of the conflict. It has the further attraction of describing the little-known machinery which was set up in Canada to help Rebel soldiers who had escaped Northern prisons make their way back to the Confederacy, by way of Nova Scotia and Bermuda.

Still, the principal attraction of this account is human rather than historic. It does not add appreciably to the monumental store of information which scholars have accumulated on this conflict.

Decimus et Ultimus Barziza was a well-educated, well-travelled, and sophisticated observer. His account of his war experiences is realistic, with little of the sentimental flavor or stilted formality common to the writings of his period.

The paperback pocket-size book was published in Houston, in early February, 1865, in the printing establishment of Willard Richardson and James Owen. This shop was better known as the "News Job Office," the commercial printing division of the *Tri-Weekly Galveston News,* which had moved to Houston when Galveston was threatened with invasion some months earlier.

The first advertisement for the book was carried in the *News* of February 5. The publishers offered to send it postpaid to any address upon receipt of one dollar, specie. In none of the several advertisements which appeared in the *News* and the *Houston Tri-Weekly Telegraph* in February of 1865 was the name of the author given. Nor did it appear in the book. How Dr. Winkler identified the work as Barziza's is unknown. His identification was confirmed, however, by this writer in 1962 when he discovered a second copy in the possession of James H. Barziza, Sr., 909 West 23rd Street, Houston. This grand-nephew of D. U. Barziza had inherited his copy from his father, who had been a member of the D. U. Barziza household. This was the author's personal copy. When he had it bound in 1875, his by-line was printed, with the title, on the cover.

In editing this memoir I have attempted to insert only such corrective or identifying information as was necessary and to make only such annotation as seemed required for a full understanding of the story. It is hoped that none of the flavor of Barziza's original has been lost.

A few notes include no references. These deal with such subjects as the general action at Gettysburg on which such a multiplicity of sources is available that a listing would be tedious. Such notes are included only to refresh the reader's memory on information with which he is assumed to be already familiar.

For a similar reason the Introduction, giving something of Barziza's military record from the time he entered the Confederate service until the opening of his memoir, has been held to personal rather than general information. The story of the Texans who made up Hood's Brigade, and the Fourth Texas Infantry in particular, has been told in full in such excellent memoirs as Nicholas A. Davis' *Campaign from Texas to Maryland*, Joseph B. Polley's *Hood's Texas Brigade* and *A Soldier's Letters to Charming Nellie*, Val. C. Giles' *Rags and Hope*, compiled and edited by Mary Lasswell, and John Bell Hood's *Advance and Retreat*. A more recent book, Colonel Harold B. Simpson's *Gaines Mill to Appomattox*, covers in detail the experiences of the men of Company E of the Fourth Texas Infantry, which during this period were almost identical with those of Barziza's Company C.

Since the original of *Adventures of a Prisoner of War* was published anonymously and because few latter-day Texans have even heard of the colorful and competent man who wrote this book, inclusion of a brief biographic sketch of Decimus et Ultimus Barziza seemed proper. Some of the material in this sketch has appeared in articles by the editor, published in the *Houston Post*, the *Texas Bar Journal*, and the *Southwestern Historical Quarterly*, but a considerable portion has come to light since these publications.

The editor is indebted to James M. Day, archivist, Texas State Library, for permission to make a photocopy of the text for a work copy, and to Mr. Day and his staff for their aid in locating much Barziza material in their files. The helpful suggestions and assistance given by the staff of the Barker History Center and the Archives Division of The University of Texas Library should also be acknowledged. Mr. Thomas Townsend, of Austin, was most gracious in allowing the use of letters from the papers of his grandfather, Captain William Purnell Townsend. Mr. Morton Brown, also of Austin, very generously made available the personal address book and memoir which his father, the late First Lieutenant William Morton Brown, compiled while he was a prisoner at Johnson's Island.

The greatest help in coming to know and understand the truly remarkable Texan who wrote these memoirs was offered by James H. Barziza, Sr. This kindly gentleman is the son of the late Phillip Dorsey Barziza, nephew and "adopted son" of Decimus et Ultimus. From his father James H. Barziza inherited a strong affection for his illustrious "Uncle Dessie" and a thorough knowledge of his life and character, which he readily shared with me.

Finally, the editor acknowledges with deep gratitude the invaluable assistance of Bertrand B. Baker and Mrs. Garland Coker, both of the staff of the Texana Program of The University of Texas, in the final preparation of the manuscript.

R. Henderson Shuffler

CONTENTS

Preface ix

Decimus et Ultimus Barziza 3

Introduction 19

The Adventures of a Prisoner of War 33

Bibliography 127

Index 131

ILLUSTRATIONS

Frontispiece

Decimus et Ultimus Barziza, Fifteenth Legislature, 1875

Following page 66

Title Page of Original Diary

War-Time Sketch of Johnson's Island

Following page 82

Portrait of Decimus et Ultimus Barziza

Barziza Family Plot in Houston, Texas

DECIMUS ET ULTIMUS BARZIZA

Biography

Introduction

DECIMUS ET ULTIMUS BARZIZA

Despite its remoteness from the older cultural centers, Texas has been, from its beginnings, remarkably cosmopolitan, both in population and attitude. Early Texans were unimpressed by such titles as those of the soldier-politician, Felipe Henrique Neri, Baron de Bastrop, or the colonizer, Carl Braunfels, Prince of Solms. Many of them considered the effete French envoy, Count Alphonse de Saligny, downright ridiculous. There has always been more of an inclination to ask, in Texas, how red a man's blood might be, rather than how blue.

It was quite natural that the impressive genealogical background of the Barziza brothers was ignored when they came to Texas in the mid-nineteenth century, and either forgotten or accepted quite casually by their Texas descendants. This background would not be recalled now, except for the fact that Decimus et Ultimus, youngest of the Barzizas, wrote the name in bold strokes across the pages of Texas history of the Civil War and Reconstruction periods.

Decimus et Ultimus Barziza was the product of a notable lineage, including some of the most distinguished families of Italy, England, and colonial America. The first of his antecedents on the American scene had appeared in tidewater Virginia, in the seventeenth century. They were the Philip Ludwells, I, II, and III, who became the largest landholders in the rich plantation country along the James River.[1]

Philip Ludwell III (1716–1767), master of Green Spring, Rich Neck, and Chippokes plantations, near Williamsburg, was

[1] Much of the material which follows is taken directly from "Decimus et Ultimus Barziza," by R. Henderson Shuffler, *Southwestern Historical Quarterly*. LXVI, No. 4 (April, 1963), 501–512, and from "A Texas Profile: Decimus et Ultimus Barziza," by R. Henderson Shuffler, *Texas Bar Journal*, Vol. XXVI, No. 4 (April 22, 1963), pp. 303–304, 344–346.

the third of his name to serve in the Virginia colony's House of Burgesses, on the vestry of Williamsburg's Bruton Parish Church, and on the Governor's Council. He was the most valued assistant of colonial Governor Robert Dinwiddie in dealing with the Indians, and was largely responsible for Dinwiddie's appointment of his young friend, George Washington, as commander of the Virginia militia in 1755.[2]

Philip Ludwell's daughter, Lucy, married John Paradise, noted English scholar, in 1769.[3] Paradise, born in Macedonia, of an English father and a Greek mother, was the most accomplished linguist in England in his day, a member of the Royal Society of London, and an intimate of Boswell, Johnson, and other leading English men of science and letters. Close friends of the couple in America included Benjamin Franklin and Thomas Jefferson, as well as Lucy's kinsmen, George Washington, Light Horse Harry Lee, the Byrds, and the Burrs.[4]

After the death of John Paradise in 1795, Lucy Ludwell returned to her ancestral lands, refurbished and reoccupied what is now known as the Ludwell-Paradise house in Williamsburg,[5] and lived there in considerable splendor until her increasing eccentricities caused her to be committed to the Eastern Lunatick Hospital. There she died in 1814.

[2] A. B. Shepperson, *John Paradise and Lucy Ludwell of London and Williamsburg*, p. 21.

[3] "A marriage contract, made in 1769, between John Paradise and Lucy Ludwell . . . is still in possession of their descendants, now residents of Houston, Texas—in a good state of preservation . . ." (anonymous, *History of Texas Together with a Biographical History of the Cities of Houston and Galveston*, p. 348). J. H. Barziza, Sr., 909 West 23rd, Houston, told R. H. Shuffler, in an interview September 15, 1962, that a trunk full of family papers, believed to have included this contract, were taken out by a maid and burned, after the death of Phillip Henry Barziza, son of William Lee Barziza, in 1939.

[4] Shepperson, *John Paradise and Lucy Ludwell*, pp. 403, 454–456; Julian P. Boyd (ed.), *The Papers of Thomas Jefferson*, Vols. 9–12.

[5] This name was assigned the house by the Williamsburg Restoration, in spite of the fact that John Paradise never lived in it.

John and Lucy Ludwell Paradise were survived by a daughter, Lucy, who had been married to Count Antonio Barziza of Venice, in London, in 1787. Of this marriage, Viscount Filippo Ignacio Barziza was born in 1796.[6]

Upon the death of his grandmother, the Viscount came to America to claim his inheritance. Her personal property was turned over to him, but he found that in order to claim her lands he would be required to renounce his Italian title and to become an American citizen. This he did, filing suit for the lands against two cousins who had taken them over.[7] Even with the advice and the aid of Thomas Jefferson, who was by this time President of the United States, he lost the lawsuit.

Litigation had eaten away most of his inheritance of personal property. Plain Phillip Ignatius Barziza, American citizen, married a Williamsburg girl from a distinguished French-Canadian family,[8] Cecelia Amanda Bellett,[9] and settled down in Williamsburg to make the most of his situation. He found employment as a keeper at the Eastern Lunatick Hospital, where his grandmother had spent her last days.

There was no particular onus to working at the asylum. It was the town's principal institution. As a matter of fact, Williamsburg, in those days, was known locally as "the town where the lazy look after the crazy." [10]

Ignatius was not too lazy, however. His and Cecelia's family

[6] Shepperson, *John Paradise and Lucy Ludwell*, pp. 456.

[7] *Ibid.*, p. 447.

[8] *History of Texas* (p. 348) says her father was a native of France, a royalist who fled when Robespierre came to power and who settled in Canada, "where he changed his name from Lord Clairmount to Bellett." In Canada he married the daughter of the governor general. They later moved to Williamsburg, where Cecelia was born.

[9] They were married in 1818, according to data on family tombstone, Glenwood Cemetery, Houston (*History of Texas*, p. 348). The tombstone lists name as Cecelia Bellett; *History of Texas*, as Cecelia Amanda Bellett; Shepperson, as Cecile Belette.

[10] Shepperson, *John Paradise and Lucy Ludwell*, p. 447.

grew at an amazing pace, considering that they were Episcopalians. When the tenth little Barziza arrived, Ignatius is said to have gone to one of Williamsburg's numerous taverns to celebrate. He admitted to a friend, quite dolefully, that he had used up all of the fine old family names, like Paradise, Ludwell, Lee, and Fitzhugh, and was at a loss as to what to christen his latest.

"How many had you already?" his friend is reported to have asked.

"Nine."

"Is this a boy or a girl?"

"Boy."

"Then, damn it all, Barziza, name him Decimus et Ultimus, and make it so!" the friend exploded.[11]

The youngster was christened, and became the "Tenth and Last" Barziza of his generation.

Ignatius managed to send all of his sons who reached maturity to the local College of William and Mary. An older son, Francis Louis, graduated with a law degree in 1843, and promptly moved to Texas.[12] He set up at the thriving town of Wheelock, in Robertson County, and became a widely known and respected attorney.[13] (He changed his name, of course, to Frank.)[14]

The younger brothers, William Lee, Phillip Ignatius, Jr., and Decimus et Ultimus, followed F. L. Barziza to Texas. The

[11] *Ibid.*, p. 448.

[12] *History of Texas*, p. 348.

[13] *The Dallas Herald,* July 10, 1858, listed F. L. Barziza of Wheelock as "V Em." among officers of the Grand Commandery, Knights Templar, of Texas for the ensuing year. *The Dallas Herald,* February 2, 1859, reported F. L. Barziza "One of several gentlemen being urged for appointment as Reporter for the Supreme Court of Texas."

[14] *The Dallas Herald,* February 2, 1859, "our old friend, Frank Barziza."

first two, after a brief stay at Wheelock, moved to Chambers County, where they became successful planters.[15]

When Decimus et Ultimus arrived in Texas in 1857, he had just received his bachelor of arts degree from William and Mary. His older brothers sent him to Independence, where he enrolled at Baylor University to study law under Bible-toting, fiddle-playing Judge R. E. B. Baylor. In 1859 he took his law degree [16] and began his practice at the new Robertson County seat of Owensville, five miles north of the present town of Franklin.[17]

Two years later, when the Civil War drums began to roll, Decimus et Ultimus Barziza volunteered. He was commissioned a first lieutenant of the Fourth Texas Infantry, C.S.A., in what later was to be known as Hood's Brigade.[18] He was later promoted to captain, was twice wounded in action, and was taken prisoner at the Battle of Gettysburg. He spent a year in Federal hospitals and in prison at Johnson's Island, before he made his escape by diving through the window of a moving train one night, near Huntingdon, Pennsylvania. Making his way to Canada, he was one of the first Confederate escapees to use the mechanism set up by friendly Canadians and Confederate representatives for the return of fugitive rebels to the Confederacy. He was taken from Nova Scotia to Bermuda, then, on a blockade runner, back to the South through the port of Wilmington, North Carolina.

His memoirs of these experiences, written during his convalescence from the hardships of escape, were published at Houston several months before the end of the war.

Returning to Texas, Decimus et Ultimus settled in Houston,

[15] *History of Texas,* p. 348.
[16] *Ibid.,* p. 348.
[17] W. P. Webb, H. B. Carroll *et al.* (eds.), *The Handbook of Texas,* 2 vols.
[18] *Houston Daily Post,* March 14, 1882.

where his brother, Phillip Ignatius, Jr.,[19] had served most of the war as an enrolling officer for recruits to the Fourth Texas Infantry.[20] Like thousands of other Confederate veterans, he was without funds and without a ready means to establish himself. He found work as a night clerk at the old Rusk House.[21] There he continued to study law and awaited an opportunity to establish a reputation on which to build his practice. Opportunity was not long in coming.

An old Waller County feud flared into spectacular violence in a downtown Houston office building. Colonel Kirby, an influential planter from the Hempstead area, was gunned down by Captain John Steel, a former Waller County farmer. It looked like cold-blooded murder. On investigation Barziza learned there had been a feud of long standing between these men and that Kirby had forced Steel to leave Waller County, on threat of killing him on sight. Steel had moved to Houston and was in the Wilson Building, at the corner of Main and Congress, one day on business, when his enemy visited the same floor to call on the federal commander of occupation troops. They met in a hallway and Steel opened fire. Since the dead man had been a prominent and influential citizen, the shooting attracted wide attention.

Young Barziza volunteered to defend Captain Steel. He handled the case with such skill as to attract the admiration of local lawyers, and his plea to the jury was spoken of for years

[19] Erroneously listed on the Muster Roll of the Fourth Texas Regiment, Texas Volunteers, October, 1862, as "P. J. Barzeza, Agent Texas Depot" (Donald E. Everett [ed.], *Chaplain Davis and Hood's Texas Brigade,* p. 204). In this roster he is shown as present with Company C, fighting as a private, at the second battle of Manassas, and the rest of the time absent on other duties.

[20] Official notices, published in the *Houston Tri-Weekly Telegraph,* April 12, 1865, and at other times throughout the war, are signed "P. I. Barziza, Captain, Enrolling Officer."

[21] Benajah H. Carroll, *Standard History of Texas From a Study of the Original Sources,* p. 111.

as the most eloquent speech ever made in the Harris County Courthouse. In spite of the best efforts of the prosecutor and two able lawyers employed to assist him, the jury, after brief deliberation, returned a verdict of "not guilty." Barziza's reputation was made.[22]

The meteoric career of the fiery young lawyer was almost blighted at its start. In June of 1867 he became embroiled in a bitter quarrel with Colonel C. C. Gillespie, crusading editor of the *Houston Daily Telegraph*. Gillespie, in print,[23] accused Barziza of soliciting, on a contingent fee basis, the claims of Central Texas cotton farmers against the Houston & Texas Central Railway Company, for alleged overcharges on hauling cotton. He accused the lawyer of "Champerty, Maintenance and Barratry."

The next day Barziza replied with a query as to whether Colonel Gillespie would be willing to accept a challenge "for personal and honorable redress." [24] He stated that he took the precautionary step of making such an inquiry before issuing a challenge "because I do not desire . . . that I should be brought under the operation of the dueling oath,[25] by sending a challenge which probably might not be accepted."

Gillespie brushed off the query with the statement that "Captain Barziza knows very well that the editor of the *Telegraph*

[22] *Ibid.*, p. 112.

[23] *Houston Daily Telegraph*, June 25, 1867.

[24] Barziza's letter and Gillespie's comments were published in the *Houston Daily Telegraph* of June 27, 1867.

[25] A provision prohibiting duelists from becoming officeholders in Texas passed as a law of the Republic, January 18, 1840; it was incorporated into the Texas Constitution of 1845, and was a part of the basic law of Texas for many years. Until January 1, 1939, all state officials were required to take oaths that they had never issued or accepted a challenge, or taken part in a duel (W. R. Hogan, "Rampant Individualism in the Republic of Texas," *Southwestern Historical Quarterly*, XLIV, No. 4 [April, 1941], p. 473).

is under bond of $3,000, to keep the peace, brought about by the enmity to him of Federal Col. DeGress . . ." [26]

As is usually the case when a man outside the newspaper profession becomes engaged in a controversy in print with the editor of a newspaper, Barziza found himself somewhat at a disadvantage. In the *Telegraph* of June 28 Gillespie reported that his opponent had been "hunting around town to find a printing office which would print him some handbills, posting the editor of the *Telegraph* as a coward for not accepting a challenge which Capt. Barziza never sent." Jeeringly, the editor offered to print the handbills or to insert their contents, as an item of news, in his columns.

To this taunt Barziza replied with a letter [27] informing the editor that he had freed him of his peace bond by depositing $3,000 with the district clerk. "I now desire to know of you," he wrote, "whether you are willing to listen to any proposals, if made to you, by which you may place yourself in a position to be personally attacked by me, without endangering the lives of persons on the streets, and so that the officers of the law may not be likely to interfere."

At this point mutual friends intervened, declaring both parties at fault to some degree, and persuading them to call the

[26] Jacob C. DeGress, born in Cologne, Prussia, immigrated to Missouri as a child. He enlisted in the Third Missouri Infantry, U.S. Army, and rose to rank of lieutenant colonel. In June, 1865, he came to Texas as an assistant commissioner of the Freedman's Bureau for the Eastern District of Texas. Although mustered out in September, 1866, he continued to live in Houston and work with the Freedman's Bureau in Texas and in Louisiana until rejoining the U.S. Army July 28, 1867, as a first lieutenant in the Ninth Cavalry. He retired December 31, 1870, became mayor of Austin, 1877–1878, and served as chairman of the State Republican Committee, 1888–1900 (*The Handbook of Texas*).

[27] Letter dated June 28, published in the *Houston Daily Telegraph*, July 2, 1867.

whole thing off. Barziza and Gillespie published stiff letters of retraction, and the quarrel ended.[28]

As Radical rule of Texas became increasingly oppressive under Reconstruction, Barziza reacted characteristically by taking more of an interest in Democratic affairs. He joined Ashbel Smith, J. P. Henderson, F. R. Lubbock, and others in calling a "conservative State convention," to be held in the Harris County Courthouse on January 20, 1868.[29] In July he was serving as a member of the state-wide committee which organized the State Democratic Convention at Bryan.[30]

When the Democrats regained control of Texas in 1873, Barziza's political star rose. He was elected to the Fourteenth Legislature as a representative from Harris County and occupied a strong position in the group surrounding Governor-Elect Richard Coke.

Scalawag Governor Edmund J. Davis, who had been defeated in the Democratic landslide of 1873, refused to recognize the legality of the election and barricaded himself in the basement of the Capitol. The Democrats took over the second floor and set about the business of organizing the new government. Davis filled his sector of the Capitol with armed state troops, mostly Negroes. The Democrats countered by stationing the Travis Rifles on the second floor and surrounding the building with other armed guards.

In this tense situation Barziza was appointed to a joint House-Senate committee of six members to consider the Governor's message refusing to acknowledge the election. Davis had offered

[28] Statement of mediators W. P. Hill, M. S. Munson, X. B. DeBray, B. D. Chenowath, E. H. Cushing, and C. C. Hearne, as well as letters of retraction by Barziza and Gillespie published in *Houston Daily Telegraph,* July 2, 1867. Adjustment of the difficulty was also reported in *The Dallas Herald,* July 13, 1867.

[29] *The Dallas Herald,* January 11, 1868.

[30] *The Dallas Herald,* July 18, 1868.

a compromise. He would leave it up to the Federal government to determine which legislature and which set of Texas officials it would recognize.[31] Barziza's committee refused to accept these terms and the next day (January 14) it named a subcommittee to wait on the Secretary of State and to secure the election returns for canvassing.[32] Secretary of State James Newcombe refused to deliver the returns unless ordered to do so by Governor Davis.

On receipt of this message the House named a committee of seven, with Barziza as chairman, to "canvass the returns by any means practicable, and report the results."[33] Barziza drew up a letter, calling on Governor Davis to instruct his Secretary of State to hand over the election returns. He delivered this letter in person, in the Governor's well-guarded basement office. Davis told him that he did not think the new legislature was entitled to the returns, but that if Barziza would go to the office of the Secretary of State and take them, he would not be resisted. Barziza went. Newcombe pointed out the returns, spread on a table, and Barziza took them. Newcombe then drew up a note, stating that the returns had been taken under protest; Barziza signed it, with three clerks signing as witnesses.[34]

A joint session of the House and Senate met at 3:30 that afternoon to canvass the votes. By midnight the count had been completed, and Richard Coke inaugurated as governor, with R. B. Hubbard as lieutenant governor. Barziza was one of the committee named to escort Coke to the rostrum for his inaugural address, around midnight.

A contemporary historian described Decimus et Ultimus Barziza, as he was at this period, as "black-eyed, black-haired

[31] *Galveston Daily News,* January 14, 1874. Original of Davis' message in Texas State Archives.

[32] *Galveston Daily News,* January 15, 1874.   [33] *Ibid.*

[34] *Galveston Daily News,* January 16, 1874. Original of note in Texas State Archives. George Clark, in his memoirs, *A Glance Backward, or, Some Events in the Past History of My Life,* gives a briefer, but similar, account.

and of Italian descent; he was bright, energetic, eloquent and heterogeneous . . . fiery, impetuous, bold, quick and ready of speech, with a clear, ringing voice and the dramatic quality highly developed." He was said to have been addressed generally by his intimates and professional associates as "Bar." [35]

In the Fourteenth Legislature Barziza took the lead in seeking to call a convention for a new state constitution [36] and was active in the work of rewriting the restrictive laws which had been placed on the Texas statutes by a succession of Reconstruction legislatures.

Late in 1875 he was re-elected by the voters of Harris County [37] and at the opening of the Fifteenth Legislature he was a strong contender for the speakership.[38] He lost the speakership to T. R. Bonner of Smith County on a vote of forty-five to forty-three.[39]

During the Fifteenth Legislature Barziza and a strong minority group clashed bitterly with the majority over a bill [40] designed to give the Texas & Pacific Railway Company an extension of time for complying with requirements for a land grant.[41] The bill had passed the Senate amid cries of "railroading" and rumors of palm-greasing on July 25, 1876. Unable to secure passage in the House before noon, July 31, 1876, the date set by joint resolution for adjournment, proponents of the bill

[35] Norman G. Kittrell, *Governors Who Have Been and Other Public Men of Texas*, p. 84.

[36] *The Dallas Herald,* January 24, 1874, and February 13, 1875.

[37] *The Dallas Herald,* December 25, 1875.

[38] ". . . we know of none more competent to fill the speaker's chair than the Honorable D. U. Barziza . . . an excellent lawyer, fine parliamentarian, and quick, forceable and energetic speaker" (*The Dallas Herald,* March 11, 1876).

[39] *House Journal,* 15th Texas Legislature, p. 4.

[40] Senate Bill 303, "An Act for the Relief of Railroads and other Internal Improvement Companies."

[41] *House Journal,* 15th Texas Legislature, p. 733.

attempted to keep the Legislature in session beyond that time in order to keep the measure alive.[42]

The original sine die adjournment resolution was rescinded by the Senate. An attempt to do the same in the House was blocked by Barziza and his friends. On the morning of July 31 a resolution was introduced, calling for adjournment until 3:30 that afternoon. Barziza rose to speak, declaring that the session would end at noon, in accordance with the original resolution. He refused to resume his seat until forcibly seated by the sergeant at arms. The resolution carried.[43]

When the Legislature resumed session at 3:30 that afternoon Barziza and thirty-three others were absent, making it impossible to secure a quorum. The number of absentees increased to thirty-five on August 1, and the Speaker ordered the sergeant at arms to arrest the missing members and bring them in. Barziza never returned. On August 2 he was reported sick in his rooms, and on that day his formal resignation was read to the House.[44]

---

[42] There were other pressing reasons for keeping the Legislature in session (set out in Governor Richard Coke's message, read to the House on July 31), but Barziza and his group believed that the entire maneuver was aimed at giving the railroad an undue advantage.

[43] *House Journal,* 15th Texas Legislature, p. 730.

[44] It appears in the *House Journal* on page 734:

On account of my health, and believing that the first and regular session of the 15th Legislature was lawfully adjourned at twelve o'clock on Monday the 31st of July, and believing that the Speaker of the House should have so held and declared, I hereby resign my place as a member of the 15th Legislature, that place being a member of the House from Harris County.

In severing my connection from the House, I beg to say that I carry with me no feelings or animosities which may have been temporarily engendered in acrimonious debate; but I tender to the officers and members of this House, personally, assurances of kind feelings and respect, and request that this document may be spread upon your journals.

D. U. BARZIZA

Four other minority members [45] resigned the same day, but the remainder of the group stayed to fight the railroad bill. It was not allowed to come up again during the session, which ran until noon, August 21.

This was the end of Barziza's political career, although, in 1878, he was touted for the lieutenant-governorship by the *Houston Age*.[46] He returned to Houston, where his business interests and law practice fully occupied his time.

On May 1, 1875, Decimus et Ultimus Barziza and five other Houston lawyers had organized what is said to be [47] Texas' oldest trust organization, the Houston Land and Trust Company.[48] Other organizers, and members of the board, were J. C. Hutcheson, Colonel W. B. Botts, Judge E. P. Hill, Colonel J. B. Likens, and Judge James Masterson. Barziza was chairman of the board. The company was chartered to buy and sell lands and act in all matters of trust.

Beginning with a capital stock of $100,000, the firm set up for business at the northwest corner of Main and Franklin, in Houston. It is reported they opened with only $6,000 in cash.[49] Barziza was quite active in the affairs of the thriving business.

In addition, he was in great demand as a criminal lawyer. In spite of a tendency to stutter in general conversation, he was fiery and eloquent at the bar. A nephew, Phillip Dorsey Barziza, told his children [50] of how, as a child, he was taken to court to hear his "Uncle Dessie" plead a case. He said that on this occa-

[45] E. A. Perrenot, W. M. Rust, H. R. Von Biberstein, and L. F. Roberts.

[46] *Austin Weekly Statesman,* February 28, 1878.

[47] *Houston Chronicle,* May 1, 1940.

[48] Records of organization in files of Houston Bank and Trust Company, Houston, Texas.

[49] *Houston Chronicle,* May 1, 1940.

[50] J. H. Barziza, Sr., 909 West 23rd Street, Houston (son of late P. D. Barziza, Sr.), to R. H. Shuffler, September 16, 1962.

sion "Uncle Dessie" was so eloquent and convincing that the prosecutor, in effect, withdrew, and the jury decided for acquittal without leaving the box.

After such trials it was customary for the lawyers to gather at a bar, or in a private home, and to celebrate their joys in victory or to drown their sorrows in defeat. According to family stories, Decimus et Ultimus participated in these celebrations with great enthusiasm. The only way his wife [51] could persuade him to leave the party and come home was to send his small nephew, Phillip, whom they had adopted and whom the lawyer adored, for him. It is told [52] that little Phillip would go in to his uncle and say: "Uncle Dessie, it is time to go home."

The uncle would invariably reply: "All right, little man, let's go," setting down his bottle and taking his leave.

Decimus et Ultimus Barziza died at his home at the corner of San Jacinto and Walnut Streets, in Houston, on January 30, 1882, "after a lingering illness." [53] He was then forty-three years of age. He was buried with full honors from Harmony Lodge No. 861, Knights of Honor, and Webb Encampment No. 13, I.O.O.F. [54] Pallbearers were prominent members of the Houston Bar. [55] Burial was in the Barziza family plot, [56] in Glenwood Cemetery.

[51] Former Patricia Nicholas of Buckingham County, Virginia, whom he married in March, 1869.

[52] J. H. Barziza, Sr., told R. H. Shuffler, September 16, 1962, that his father, the late P. D. Barziza, Sr., who was the nephew and "adopted son" of D. U. Barziza, often told him these stories.

[53] *The Galveston Daily News,* January 31, 1882.

[54] J. H. Barziza, Sr., says that the Houston Light Guards, which D. U. had commanded, also attended en masse.

[55] J. C. Hutcheson, E. P. Hill, W. C. Oliver, S. Taliaferro, W. B. Botts, Major M. Looscan, J. W. Jones, and E. P. Turner.

[56] Graves in the Barziza family plot include the following: Phillip Ignatius, Sr., born Venice, Italy, 8–10–1796, died Houston, Texas, 3–25–1875; Cecelia Amanda Bellett, born Williamsburg, Virginia, 9–8–

The individual headstone over his grave, below the customary name and dates, bears an inscription which well sums up the career of this colorful Texan:

Although his career was brief, he was distinguished among his fellow men as a gallant soldier, a wise legislator, and a brilliant and learned lawyer. He possessed, in the highest degree the grand qualities of human nature:

Honor, Genius and Enthusiasm.

In the spring term of District Court of Harris County, in 1882, Major Michael Looscan read a glowing tribute to Barziza, whom he described as "an able and accomplished lawyer." He concluded with this statement: "I never knew a man that surpassed him in those grand qualities of human conduct, honor and courage, qualities that eagle-plume men's souls and fit them for the fiercest sun."

This eulogy was printed in full in the *Houston Daily Post* and other Texas newspapers and reprinted, with appropriate comments, in the 1883 edition of *Burke's Texas Almanac and Immigrant's Handbook.*[57] A portrait of the distinguished lawyer

---

1797, died Houston, 6–8–1872; Decimus et Ultimus, born Williamsburg, 9–4–1838, died Houston, 1–30–1882; Francis Louis, born Williamsburg, 4–5–1822, died Chambers County, Texas, 2–4–1862; William Lee, born Williamsburg, 12–8–1824, died Chambers County, 11–16–1878; Sarah Mountcastle, consort of W. L., born Charles City County, Virginia, 3–5–1827, died Chambers County, 4–9–1880; Phillip Ignatius, Jr., born Williamsburg, 6–9–1836, died Houston, 7–15–1872; Phillippa Ludwell, born Williamsburg, 1820, died Houston, 7–25–1898; Phillip Dorsey, son of Phillip Ignatius, Jr., born Houston, 9–8–1872, died Houston, 1948. The central monument in the plot notes also that one son of Ignatius and Cecelia Barziza, Edgar Athling, born in Williamsburg, 3–29–1826, died in California, 9–25–1882, and is buried there, and that four children who died as infants, Edgar Antonio, John Paradise, James Lee, and Lucy Ludwell, were buried in Bruton Parish churchyard, Williamsburg.

[57] J. Burke (ed.), *Burke's Texas Almanac and Immigrant's Handbook for 1883*, p. 127.

hangs today in the Jury Assembly Room of the Harris County Civil Courts Building.[58] The city of Houston has a Barziza Street,[59] and nine Barzizas, descendants of a brother, are listed in the Houston directory.[60] Decimus et Ultimus Barziza left his mark on Texas.

[58] A portrait of D. et U. Barziza hung for many years in the Harris County Courthouse. When the courthouse was renovated, to become the Harris County Civil Courts Building, the old portraits from the county "Hall of Fame" were retouched and reframed. They now hang in the Jury Assembly Room. Of a score of these, only four were for years unidentified. One of the unlabeled portraits has been recently identified as that of Barziza.

[59] This street, in an area where D. et U. Barziza once owned much property, runs two blocks, from Stonewall Cemetery, north, to Harrisburg Road.

[60] C. R., 821 Yale; C. W., 9230 Westview; Don W., 10806 Old Katy Road; E. H., Jr., 1922 Wycliffe; G. M., 7869 Pecan Villas Road; H. D., 8830 Bunningham; J. H., Sr., 909 West 23rd; P. Dorsey, 3906 Brookwoods; Robert A., 7702 Brykerwoods. All are descendants of Phillip Ignatius Barziza, Jr.

Of the ten children of Phillip Ignatius and Amanda B. Barziza, only two had issue. Neither of the children of William L. Barziza married; a daughter died at age fourteen and a son, Phillip Henry (1852–1939), was a bachelor. Phillip Ignatius, Jr., had one son, Phillip Dorsey, Sr., whose five sons carried on the line. These were Phillip D., Jr., Houston, Texas; Edward H., Sr., Asheville, North Carolina; Phillip H., Sr., Wellesley, Massachusetts; James H., Sr., Houston; and C. Wenzel, Houston. All are living except Edward H., Sr., who died in 1954.

INTRODUCTION

On May 3, 1861, two months and two days after Texas was formally admitted to the Confederacy, the first volunteers from Robertson County met at the county seat of Owensville and organized the "Robertson Five-Shooters."[1] This was a state militia infantry company, armed with Colt's Improved Patented five-shooting rifles.

The young Brazos-bottom planters, farmhands, clerks, and business and professional men who made up the company elected as their captain the well-known planter from Sterling,[2] William Purnell Townsend. Captain Townsend was experienced in military matters, having served as a lieutenant under Jefferson Davis in the Mexican War.[3] He was already well known to many of the Brazos planters, having come to Texas, as they had, from Mississippi.

For first lieutenant the Five-Shooters elected a promising young lawyer from the county seat, who had made many friends in the area through his easy conviviality, and who was beginning to acquire a reputation as a lawyer of ability. His name was

[1] Muster Roll, Capt. William P. Townsend's Co., Texas Infantry, undated.

[2] Named for Sterling Clack Robertson, *empresario* of the colony which covered this portion of Central Texas. The town, located on the Brazos near the present site of Calvert, has long since disappeared.

[3] Richard Denny Parker (Nona Clement Parker, ed.), *Historical Recollections of Robertson County, Texas*, p. 202. William P. Townsend was a lieutenant in Company K, First Mississippi Infantry, of which Colonel Jefferson Davis was commander, during the Mexican War.

Decimus et Ultimus Barziza, although to most of his comrades he was known as D. U. Barziza, or simply "Bar."

Through May and June the volunteers trained at a campground near Block House Spring in adjoining Milam County,[4] collected equipment, and awaited orders. Early in July they marched down the Brazos to the railhead at Millican and boarded the Houston & Texas Central Railway cars for Camp Earl Van Dorn, near Harrisburg. There twenty such volunteer companies were being formed as the first contingent of Texas troops to be sent to the fighting front in Virginia.

At Camp Van Dorn, on July 15, 1861, Lieutenant D. U. Barziza, with the other officers and with some of the men from Captain Townsend's company, formally enlisted in the Confederate service for the duration of the war.[5] A number of the Robertson County volunteers, like those from other areas, turned back home at this point. They had originally enlisted under the call of Governor Clark for a term of one year. When the Confederacy refused to accept enlistments for less than "during the war," the men became disgruntled and withdrew.[6] Many of them were already unhappy because the Confederacy had served notice that it did not need any more cavalry at this time, and, as a result, they must go as foot-soldiers. Texans, raised on horseback, resented the idea of being expected to do their fighting on foot.[7]

[4] *Ibid.,* p. 203.

[5] Muster Roll, Capt. William P. Townsend's Co., Texas Infantry, in printed note, states: "The commissioned officers and some of the men subsequently enlisted . . . for the war."

[6] Mary Lasswell, compiler and editor of *Rags and Hope: The Memoirs of Val C. Giles,* describes this situation in relation to another company of the organization which later became the Fourth Texas Regiment.

[7] George B. Erath (dictated to Lucy A. Erath), *Memoirs of Major George B. Erath,* p. 96.

There were other reasons for dissatisfaction by this time. Camp Van Dorn was located in a wooded area which the Reverend Nicholas Davis described as "a low, miasmic, unhealthy region." [8] Many of the men were sick. They were impatient, too, to get on to the front. They had joined to fight Yankees, not to slog through the rain on a muddy drill field. They were short on camp equipment—the supplies promised by the Confederacy had been late in arriving—and were irritated by the necessity of learning to cook their own meals and to wash their own clothes.[9] To make matters worse, they had received no pay.[10]

Lieutenant Barziza and his comrades were jubilant when word finally came that they would be moving out for Virginia on August 16. They were in high spirits as they boarded the train at Harrisburg for the first leg of their journey. There were four companies in this first group to leave Texas. With Captain Townsend's "Robertson Five-Shooters" rode Captain J. C. G. Key's "Hardeman Rifles" from Goliad County, Captain Benjamin F. Carter's "Tom Green Rifles" from Travis County, and Captain J. P. Bane's "Knights of Guadalupe" from Guadalupe County. Captain Key, as senior officer, commanded the contingent of approximately five hundred.[11]

The trip from Camp Van Dorn to Virginia was in some respects one of the bitterest experiences of the war for Barziza and his men. It took a total of twenty-seven days and involved travel by train, boat, cart, and on foot. It was the walking, or

[8] Nicholas A. Davis, *Campaign from Texas to Maryland, with the Battle of Sharpsburg,* p. 7.

[9] Colonel Harold B. Simpson, *Gaines Mill to Appomattox: Waco & McLennan County in Hood's Texas Brigade,* p. 38.

[10] Muster Roll, Capt. William P. Townsend's Co., July 15 through August 31, 1861, shows August 31 as the first payment date of this company.

[11] Simpson, *Gaines Mill to Appomattox,* p. 43.

more correctly, the wading—through some 135 miles of swamp-land in Louisiana—which they never forgot. In that "track of country which will bog the shadow of a flying buzzard," as one soldier described it,[12] they abandoned their supplies, their guns, and much of their uniforms. In the morass of the Louisiana swamplands they threw off their coats, pants, and shoes. As Chaplain Davis later wrote, ". . . it was a common spectacle on the road to see a manly specimen of human nature trudging along, singing 'Dixie' as he went, minus everything in the shape of clothes except a shirt." [13]

At New Orleans, on August 31, they were housed in an old cotton warehouse and given new uniforms and equipment.[14] The worst of their ordeal was over. They received their first pay,[15] were given a few days to rest and enjoy the pleasures of the Crescent City, then shipped out by train for Virginia.

Barziza was happy to see again the familiar sights of his native state and to enjoy the attention drawn by his new status as a Texan. The dullness of the wait at their temporary camp in the Rocketts area on the outskirts of Richmond, from their arrival on September 12 until all of the twenty Texas companies had reported in the last of the month, was relieved by visits to familiar haunts of his boyhood as well as to the more mature attractions of the city.

In early October the Texans were moved to a new site, five miles east of Richmond, which they promptly named "Camp Texas." [16] Here they were organized into regiments and per-fected their drill. Captain Townsend's Robertson Five-Shooters lost their colorful name to become Company C, Fourth Texas Infantry Regiment. Their regiment, made up of the first ten

[12] *Ibid.,* p. 42.

[13] Davis, *Campaign from Texas to Maryland,* p. 14.

[14] Simpson, *Gaines Mill to Appomattox,* p. 48.

[15] Muster Roll, Capt. William P. Townsend's Co., July 15 through August 31, 1861.

[16] Simpson, *Gaines Mill to Appomattox,* p. 50.

companies of Texans to reach the war area, was first assigned a Texan as its commanding officer. He was Colonel R. T. P. Allen from Bastrop, president of the Military Institute there, and a stiff disciplinarian. They sent him back to Bastrop in a few days.[17] He was replaced by John Bell Hood, a Kentuckian who had seen service on the Texas frontier, and whom the men of the Fourth Texas immediately and permanently worshipped.

In early November they moved into the right wing of the Potomac line at Dumfries, where they were soon made a part of the Texas Brigade, composed of the First, Fourth, and Fifth Texas Regiments. At first under the command of Colonel Louis Wigfall, prominent Texas politician-soldier, this aggregation was soon to be headed by John Bell Hood, and to make its name in history as Hood's Texas Brigade.

The fall and winter of 1861–1862 on the Potomac line was one of dull inactivity for the Texans, with considerable illness among the men. Captain Townsend was back in Texas on a recruiting mission much of the time, and Lieutenant Barziza signed the Muster Roll in February, April, and June of 1862 as "commanding the company." [18]

In a letter to Captain Townsend in Texas, from "Camp Near Dumfries, Va.," on March 3, 1862,[19] Barziza reported: "I have been getting along smoothely and quietly. Everything goes regularly in the company and I have no trouble." In this same letter he told of preparations to move back upon Fredericksburg.

We will of course have to abandon our river batteries. We have sent off all our clothing and blankets except what each man can pack. I have in my house two days' rations of hard bread and bacon and

[17] Davis, *Campaign from Texas to Maryland,* p. 16.

[18] Muster Roll, Co. C, 4th Regiment, Texas Infantry, January-February, March-April, May-June, 1862. Simpson (*Gaines Mill to Appomattox,* Note 65, Chapter V) mentions that Townsend went home on a recruiting furlough at this time.

[19] One of Captain Townsend's letters in a collection held by his grandson, Thomas Townsend, 1108 Gaston, Austin, Texas.

2,000 extra cartridges, with orders to issue them at the word "March." We will leave all our tents and cooking utensils except frying pans and camp kettles.

Moving out, in the late spring, the Texas Brigade pulled back to the Rappahannock to hold a defensive position, waiting for the main Federal army to commit itself in a new offensive. When the offensive came it was aimed at a landing on the Yorktown Peninsula, and to this point the Texans marched to meet the enemy threat. On the afternoon of May 4 Barziza was in his old home town of Williamsburg.[20] He did not have an opportunity to tarry at old familiar sites, however. His company marched on through the town before nightfall. Two days later Barziza received his baptism of fire. His company, with the rest of the Fourth Texas, led the attack on the Federals at Eltham's Landing and won a decisive victory.[21] The enemy was driven back to its gunboats and the Rebel army continued to pull out of the Peninsula to avoid being trapped. The Fourth Texas, which had led the fight at Eltham's Landing, served as rear guard on the retreat. They held this position, and on May 12 were the last of the Confederate army to cross the swollen Chickahominy River and to take up a defensive position before Richmond.

After the indecisive Battle of Seven Pines on May 31 and June 1 the Texans did yeoman service in small patrols, probing the enemy's positions to keep him off balance and to prevent organization of an attack on the Confederate capital. On the morning of May 7 Lieutenant Barziza and Lieutenant Nash, of the Fifth Texas Regiment, were ordered to take a party of 150 men and "drive in the enemy's pickets and ascertain, as far as practical, what the main body were doing." [22]

[20] Simpson, *Gaines Mill to Appomattox*, p. 76.
[21] *Ibid.*, p. 77.
[22] Davis, *Campaign from Texas to Maryland*, p. 41.

Chaplain Davis reported [23] that

. . . they immediately proceeded to carry out his [Hood's] instructions, and attacked the Yankee outposts with such fury that they fled "pell mell," running over in their flight a Regiment of Infantry [71st Pennsylvania], which was supporting them. The regiment, thinking from indications which they saw, that at least half the "rebels" were coming, also took to their heels, and for half a mile made regular "Bull Run time." Having at length discovered that they were flying from a mere squad, they rallied, formed and opened on our boys with a will, but were so promptly answered that they dared not advance. Here, securely protected by the trees, the Texans poured an effective fire into their dense ranks, and would probably have given them another chase, had they not discovered a Yankee Regiment moving up on their left flank. This necessitated a retrograde movement, which they promptly executed, fighting front and flank as they fell back to the cover of our batteries. The enemy afterwards confessed a loss of between forty-five and fifty in this skirmish, while ours was but six killed and wounded—none missing. So successful was this foray that General Hood issued an order complimenting the men and officers.

It was in the Battle of Gaines Mill, on June 27, 1862, that Barziza became a veteran combat officer and immediately was given full command of his company with promotion to captain.[24] In this fight General Hood personally led the Fourth Texas in one of the most spectacular attacks of the war, breaching the line of McClellan's army and ending the threat of the Peninsula campaign.

[23] *Ibid.*, p. 42.
[24] Muster Roll of the Fourth Texas Regiment, prepared in October, 1862, for Chaplain N. A. Davis, published in Appendix to *Campaign from Texas to Maryland,* shows Barziza's promotion on June 27. According to the Register of the Fourth Regiment, Texas Infantry dated October 19, 1864, his promotion was granted in July, 1862. Parker (*Historical Recollections of Robertson County,* p. 131) says, incorrectly, "he was promoted on the field at Second Manassas."

25

Here the Texans acquired the title of the "Hell Roaring Fourth" and justified Hood's claim that he "could double-quick the Fourth of Texas to the gates of Hell and never break their line." [25] Here, too, the Texans took their most severe loss, with 75 killed and 180 wounded out of 40 officers and 506 men.[26]

A little more than a month later, in a letter to a friend at home,[27] Barziza gave a vivid account of the battle. As the Fourth Texas Infantry approached the battlefield on the afternoon of June 27 he wrote:

About two o'clock we could hear the roar of artillery and the rattle of musketry—incessant, fierce and continuous. . . . Closer and closer we came to the scene of the strife. Now we are in range of their artillery, though they do not see us. Shells bursting above, around, before and behind us, scattering their blazing fragments and sulphurous contents, remind us that we are now in the tide of battle. Moving slowly along, now well within the range of the batteries, a poor fellow's head is smashed right by me, and his brains scattered on his comrades near him. We move on in a run, over ditches and marshes, swamps and fences, through open fields and thick woods, up and down hill—double quicking—to the field of carnage, the harvest of death. Courier after courier arrives, urging us to hurry— our forces are hard pressed. Gen. Lee meets us, and hurries us on, as if the fate of mankind depended upon our coming. . . .

Gen. Hood and Col. [John] Marshall conduct our regiment; on we go on the run. . . . over a deep branch, meeting regiments and thousands of frightened stragglers leaving the field; some of them exclaiming as they passed us, "I wish you'd take that battery." I never dreamed of such confusion; our ranks were broken time and

[25] Simpson, *Gaines Mill to Appomattox,* p. 89.

[26] *Ibid.,* p. 89.

[27] Written from "Camp Near Richmond, Va.," August 1, 1862, and published in the *Houston Tri-Weekly Telegraph,* April 3, 1865. Apparently several copies of this letter were made. Captain William P. Townsend enclosed one with a letter to his wife, August 7, 1862 (Townsend Letters).

again by the fleeing Confederates; really the tide of battle seemed to have been rushing madly against us. Men deserted their colors, Colonels lost their commands, and God only knows how far off were a rout and a panic.

Suddenly we [Fourth Texas Regiment] faced to the front, advanced in a run up the hill, and as we reached the brow, were welcomed with a storm of grape [28] and cannister from the opposite hillside, while the two lines of infantry, protected by their works, and posted on the side of the hill, upon the top of which was placed their battery, poured deadly and staggering volleys full in our faces. Here fell our Colonel, John Marshall, and with him nearly half of his regiment. On the brow of this hill the dead bodies of our Confederate soldiers lay in numbers. They who had gone in at this point before us, and had been repulsed, stopped on this hill to fire, and were mowed down like grass. . . . When we got to the brow of the hill, instead of halting, we rushed down it, yelling, and madly plunged right into the deep branch of water at the base of the hill.

Dashing up the steep bank, being within thirty yards of the enemy's works, we flew towards the breastworks, cleared them, and slaughtered the retreating devils as they scampered up the hill towards their battery. There a brave fellow, on horseback, with his hat on his sword, tried to rally them. But they scarcely had time, even if they had been disposed, for leaping over the works, we dashed up the hill, driving them before us and capturing the battery. Thus the lines of the enemy were broken, and from that moment commenced the victory with which our arms were blessed. . . .

On we go, leaving the battery we had just taken to be held by a small party, exposed to a galling fire from the battery in front, from that on the right, and from the swarms of broken infantry all on our left and rear.

[28] Barziza was mistaken in thinking he and his companions encountered "grape," although his mistake was understandable. The best authorities on Civil War ordnance state that the Federals did not use grape, because canister was so much more effective, but a soldier on the receiving end would have had great difficulty in distinguishing the difference.

27

Yet on, on we go, with not a field officer to lead us, two-thirds of the company officers and half of the men already down—yelling, shouting, firing, running straight up to the death-dealing machines before us. . . . When we came within 300 yards of this battery, I found myself, with some others, in a lane, formed by a fence and barn, where we halted for a few seconds to blow. I could plainly see the gunners at work; down they would drive the horrid grape—a long, blazing flame issued from the pieces, and then crushing through the fence and barn, shattering rails and weatherboarding, came the terrible missiles with merciless fury. . . . When we arrived within about seventy yards of the battery, we stopped for a moment behind a very slight mound where an old fence had stood. The smoke had now settled down upon the field in thick curtains, rolling about like some half-solid substance; the dust was suffocating. We could see nothing but the red blaze of the cannon, and hear nothing but its roar and the hurtling and whizzing of the missiles. Suddenly the word is passed down the line, "Cavalry," and down came horses and riders with sabers swung over their heads, charging like an avalanche upon our scattered lines; they were met by volleys of lead, and fixed bayonets in the hands of resolute men, and in less time than I can take to write it, a squadron of U.S. regular cavalry was routed and destroyed. Horses without riders, or sometimes with a wounded or dead master dangling from the stirrups, plunged wildly and fearfully over the plain, trampling over dead and dying, presenting altogether one of the most sublime and at the same time fearful pictures that any man can conceive without being an eye-witness.

The Cavalry routed, on we rush with a yell, drive the gunners off or kill them, and our battle flag waves over the battery. . . . Our own Regiment, now a mere handful and led by Capt. Townsend, still rushed on towards the river, until ordered back for fear of being surrounded. . . . We gathered the little squad of our Regiment that was left, formed line of battle and prepared to sleep on the battlefield with the dead and dying. . . .

Thus ended the decisive battle of the 27th, which broke the right wing of the enemy and consequently caused his whole vast line to give way.

Throughout the summer of 1862 Captain Barziza led Company C, in the Battle of Malvern Hill, the skirmishes at Freeman's Ford and Thoroughfare Gap, and into Second Manassas. It was at Manassas, one of the most deadly battles of the war for the Texans, that Barziza was first wounded, taking a rifle ball in his right arm on the afternoon of August 30.[29] He was out of the fighting through October, missing the battles at Boonsboro and Antietam, but returning in time for action in the Battle of Fredericksburg, on December 13.[30]

Apparently he had returned to service too quickly, for he was back in the hospital at Richmond on January 1, and did not return to active duty until March 11.[31] He had taken part in the Siege of Suffolk, from April 11 to May 4, and was apparently completely recovered by the time of the opening of his memoirs, at the beginning of the Confederate advance which led to Gettysburg.

[29] Donald E. Everett (ed.), *Chaplain Davis and Hood's Texas Brigade,* p. 121.

[30] Muster Roll, Co. C, Fourth Texas Regiment, July-August, 1862, lists Barziza "absent—sick" on August 31. The September-October roll lists him as "Absent on furlough from wounds received at Manassas, August 30." The November-December roll lists him as "Present."

[31] Register, Medical Director's Office, Richmond, Va. (undated).

DECIMUS ET ULTIMUS BARZIZA

The Adventures of a Prisoner of War

1863–1864

THE ADVENTURES

OF A

PRISONER OF WAR

AND

Life and Scenes in Federal Prisons:

JOHNSON'S ISLAND, FORT DELAWARE,
AND POINT LOOKOUT;

BY AN ESCAPED PRISONER
Of Hood's Texas Brigade.

HOUSTON, TEXAS:
PRINTING ESTABLISHMENT—RICHARDSON & OWEN.
1865.

PREFACE.

In the following pages will be found a truthful narrative of the Adventures of a Prisoner of War. The Author was captured at the Battle of Gettysburg, Pennsylvania, and remained a prisoner until February, 1864, when he made his escape, traveled through the North to Canada, and came into the Confederacy at Wilmington, N.C.

He believes it will be read with much interest by all who have friends in captivity, and by all released prisoners. As to the disposition the critics may make of it, the character of the book is such that it will be read in spite of them, should they use it illy.

"Come one, come all, whether they laugh or cry,
The liberal Public will be sure to buy."

Chapter First.

Introductory—Preparation for the Invasive Campaign of 1863—The March Northward—Cavalry fights in the Mountains—Capture of Winchester by Ewell—Approach to the Potomac—Last night in Virginia.

N THE FOLLOWING PAGES I design to give my adventures for the past twelve months.[1] What I set down, shall be chiefly those incidents which came under my personal observation. My style may, perhaps, be objectionable, and the continued indulgence of the pronoun "I" may savor of egotism; but as this is *my book* I am writing, and *my* adventures, I am relating, I shall ask no one's pardon, and offer no apology. Many incidents herein will be well remembered by thousands of Confederate soldiers, and their recall at this time and by this means, will, I know, be agreeable and entertaining.

Early in May, 1863, the boasted Yankee army [Army of the Potomac], commanded by [Maj. Gen. Joseph] Hooker, was most shamefully beaten on the Rappahannock; and the "finest army on the planet" was, in a few days, skulking on the North bank of the River, demoralized and dispirited.[2]

---

[1] May, 1863, through June, 1864.

[2] The ebullient Barziza paints a far rosier picture than the facts justify. The corps of Stonewall Jackson had defeated the Union army under General Hooker at Chancellorsville in early May, but at a ter-

Preparations were soon after made on the part of Gen. Lee to cross the Potomac, and manœuvre Hooker out of Virginia. Accordingly, the Army was gradually withdrawn from the lower Rappahannock and was soon concentrated at or around Culpeper Court House. [Lieut. Gen. Richard S.] Ewell, with his corps, was despatched to the Valley, and the rest of the army soon followed. It was in the month of June, and old soldiers pronounced it as hot as they had ever experienced. During our march I saw scores of men lying on the road-side, who had dropped exhausted and sun-stricken, some of whom died. However, we pushed on, through sunshine and over streams, for it was a race between us and the Yankees to reach the mountain Gaps.

After less than a week's march, we crossed the Shenandoah, and held possession of Ashby's and Snicker's Gaps.

---

rific price. Jackson, accidentally wounded by his own men, on the night of May 2, had died eight days later. Now Hooker's army licked its wounds on the north side of the Rappahannock, waiting for a chance to pounce on the Confederate capital at Richmond. Lee's forces were badly scattered. Bragg was in middle Tennessee, D. H. Hill was in North Carolina, three of Pickett's brigades were at Hanover Junction, and Longstreet was in the Suffolk area with two divisions. Lee, with the remnants of his army, stood between Hooker and Richmond in the Fredericksburg area (John P. Dyer, *The Gallant Hood*, pp. 174–181).

Lee had 75,054 men available, Hooker 83,289, according to Thomas L. Livermore (*Numbers and Losses in the Civil War in America: 1861–65*, p. 140). With the South's resources dwindling, and the North's seemingly inexhaustible, Lee could not continue a stalemate on the Rappahannock indefinitely. Before Richmond he decided against dividing his forces to send two divisions to aid Bragg in Ohio and determined to invade the North instead. Lee needed supplies from the wheat fields then ripening in Pennsylvania, thought he could find a more advantageous spot to challenge Hooker, and even hoped that an invasion of Pennsylvania might create a panic in the financial centers of Philadelphia and New York (Glenn Tucker, *High Tide at Gettysburg*, pp. 19–21).

Our Cavalry here rendered most efficient service,[3] and raised themselves much in the opinion of the Infantry. They were continually fighting for weeks, and after this, no one could shout at a mounted soldier as he passed, "ten thousand dollars reward for the body of a dead Cavalryman!"

But the Infantry had their share; I think I waded the Shenandoah three times in one day. Did you ever wade a river with all your clothes on, tired, foot-sore and half mad? If so, you know how to look on the curses and complainings of an infantryman, who has to plunge in. The water was cold, the banks soft and muddy, and the bottom rocky; and I am sure I heard the earth damned by sections, and the Generals and the Army by Brigades. But, reader, if you be not a soldier, do not judge harshly of these occasional oaths from them. You don't know what it is to be tired and hungry, and really a sharp, quick and expressive oath seems to be a great relief, acting like surplus steam escaping from a safety-valve. I can but have great sympathy with profane soldiers, and their oaths, like Uncle Toby's, are scarce recorded ere they are blotted out with a tear.

Continuing our journey, we learned with much joy that Winchester and its garrison had surrendered to Ewell,[4] and all were willing to concede to him the mantle of Stonewall Jackson, if indeed, any one wore it. The country through which we passed was in full verdure, and beautiful to behold; all longed to hail the Potomac, the Rubicon of our hopes.

[3] Stuart's cavalry had defeated the Union cavalry under Pleasanton at Culpepper on June 9 (Abner Doubleday, *Gettysburg Made Plain*, p. 13). It also gave a good account of itself against a detachment of the Second Massachusetts and First New Jersey Cavalry at Ashby's Gap, July 12–20 (*The Union Army: A History of Military Affairs in the Loyal States, 1861–1865*, IV, 48). Stuart won another victory in a sharp skirmish with the Fifth Michigan Cavalry at Snicker's Gap, July 17 (*ibid.*, VI, 817).

[4] Winchester was evacuated by the Second Division, Eighth Army Corps, U.S.A., under attack by Ewell's corps, June 15, 1863 (*ibid.*, VI, 947).

On the twenty-fifth of June my Division camped within five miles or less of the Potomac, and rested here the last night on the bosom of Virginia—alas! it was the last to many a noble Southerner!

Here, near the banks of the Potomac! on the threshold of a new and untried life! Did dreamy presentiments of coming death harass that soldier who slept his last night in Virginia? Each has his hopes and his fears, and doubtless many a mother's boy sought that night to lift the veil of the future, and took a long but unwilling good-night of the old and honored State.

Many a father among those who read these lines, will say "it was *my* boy's last night in Virginia;" many a mother with tearful eye, wife, sister and loved one, all o'er the land, will often recur to this night, the last of their loved one's rest on the soil of the Old Dominion.

Yet, they sleep peacefully on the field of their glory; the heritage is yours; the mounds, rude and unmarked on the plains near Gettysburg, contain more precious relics than are beneath the lofty and labored columns erected by bigots and fanatics over the carcasses of hirelings.

Chapter Second.

Crossing of the Potomac—Reception in Maryland—All hands drunk—March towards Greencastle—Good Living—Chambersburg and the
Cumberland Valley—Gettysburg—The Battle of
July 2d—Reflections on War and Battle.

ABOUT SUN-RISE on the morning of the 26th, we
waded the river, the bands playing "My Maryland."
Cartridge boxes and Haversacks were tied on the
muzzles of the muskets, and held over and above the
shoulder, and with cheers, jokes and laughter, the boys landed
on the Williamsport side, dripping wet. The people in this place
were not very demonstrative; but many ladies saluted us with
waving 'kerchiefs. About two or three miles from Williamsport
we called a halt, drew rations of bread, meat and whiskey, and
in a short time cheerful fires were blazing, and the camp was in
an uproar of joyousness. Oh! ye, who lounge upon your easy
chairs and sip your well mixed toddies, have no conception of
the real pleasure of a "drink!" But a soldier that day, sitting
on a wet log, or leaning against a tree, with a canteen of
raw whiskey to his lips, could have told you what he thought
the "cratur" was made for. The result was that nearly all
our Division were soon "tight," and it is sincerely to be
hoped that the balance of the army succeeded in getting in the
same delectable situation. Songs were sang, speeches made, jokes
cracked, and every body was merry. Some of the boys found a

still-house near by, and filled their canteens with the liquor, not an hour old; and I know, by actual test that it made every body either sick or drunk who indulged in it. Oh! it was a glorious hour—Southern enthusiasm, hightened by Maryland whiskey. Each felt himself a host, and the sight of a brass cannon at that time would have made him mad for a charge. But, as all good things must have their ending, so did our spree; and if getting drunk was pleasant, the process of getting sober was confoundedly disagreeable; for we soon had to commence marching through the deepest and muddiest and hardest road to travel we ever footed; but we didn't regard mud and water, so long as the fire within kept blazing. After some hours, however, we were fagged and sleepy, and hungry withall. Every other man was covered with mire, and his legs dragged themselves along like some broken piece of machinery. At night, however, we camped; made good straw beds, and supped on pigs, mutton and chicken, which we *bought* from the obliging citizens around the little village of Greencastle.[1] On the morning we arose much refreshed, and prepared to continue our march towards the heart of Pennsylvania. We were, of course, objects of great curiosity to the inhabitants who had never seen an army, and were much disturbed at this Rebel invasion. Towards evening we entered the Cumberland Valley in the vicinity of Chambersburg, a neat and pretty town. In passing through Chambersburg we were greeted with many evidences of Yankee love for the "old flag," especially and chiefly on the part of the females and boys. Ladies were clothed with the stars and stripes, and had them pinned defiantly, and it must be confessed temptingly, on their *breast-works*.

"How would you like to fight under these colors," "go on,

[1] Greencastle, Pennsylvania, a few miles north of the Maryland line, en route to Chambersburg. The ironic reference to "buying" food from the "obliging" farmers refers to the fact that the farmers, under considerable pressure, were forced to accept Confederate money for their produce (John P. Dyer, *The Gallant Hood,* p. 184).

you'll catch it," and like exclamations from the females, would sometimes provoke a witty retort, but nothing insulting. I saw a fellow-soldier in passing by a little Jew on the streets, lift his hat suddenly and place his own crow's nest upon the Yankee's head; the soldier slipped in ranks and was soon lost whilst the Yank, perfectly surprised, afforded great merriment to the men. The country in this section equals any farming land I ever saw. The finest wheat it has ever been my privilege to look upon, here waved in golden splendor over hundreds of acres; and the improvement and cultivation of the soil must be carried on to perfection. The houses and yards of the people are constructed with neatness and laid out tastefully. But I was so often disappointed at the difference between the appearance of the nice dwellings and that of the inmates. Whilst looking admiringly at a sweet cottage and pretty yard, I often pictured to myself some sweet, bright-eyed creature within, when lo! a slatternly, square-faced, thick-lipped, round and clumsy looking woman would make her appearance with a pail of water on her head!

Yet, there were some very pretty girls along our route, and it cannot be denied, that there was inevitably some love making. For what can be expected of a gallant Rebel Soldier other than love making, when he finds the subject and opportunity?

Between Chambersburg and Fayetteville we remained until the evening of the first of July, and after a tedious march all night, arrived in the vicinity of Gettysburg at daylight on the second. It will be remembered that Ewell had attacked the enemy on the first, and had gained a decided advantage.[2] Now

[2] On July 1 the forces under Ewell and A. P. Hill had closed in from the north and the west on the Union First Corps under Major General Abner Doubleday and the Eleventh Corps under Major General Carl Schurz, who were aided by Buford's Cavalry. The Confederates, handicapped by the absence of their own cavalry, moved in "blind" and failed to exploit their advantage of numbers. They pushed the Union forces back through Gettysburg to a point south, where these forces occupied strong positions on Cemetery Ridge, Little Round Top and

the second day's contest was at hand. During the morning the troops were being put in position, and a calm, as of death, seemed to rest upon the earth, whilst the slow, ominous rumbling of artillery moving in position reminded us that the carnival was at hand. Everybody was confident and in the highest spirit of enthusiasm.

We were some hours getting into position, but finally formed in an open field, under the declivity of a gradually rising hill [3] in our front, upon the top of which the artillery was posted; all things ready, the batteries in our front opened, and were soon hotly engaged with the enemy's guns on the opposite heights. The enemy's shells screamed and bursted around us, inflicting considerable damage. It is very trying upon men to remain still and in ranks under a severe cannonading. One has time to reflect upon the danger, and there being no wild excitement as in a charge, he is more reminded of the utter helplessness of his present condition. The men are all flat on the ground, keeping their places in ranks, and as a shell is heard, generally try to sink themselves into the earth. Nearly every face is overspread with a serious, thoughtful air; and what thoughts, vivid and burning, come trooping up from the inner chambers of memory, the soldier can only realize.

At any rate, the long drawn cry of Attention! brought every man to his feet, and details were made to pull down the fence in our front. Every one knew what that meant, and it was really a relief to move forward. The word "Forward" was given, and

---

Round Top hills, but allowed the enemy, during the night, to bring up reinforcements sufficient to outnumber the attackers.

[3] The Texas Brigade, as a part of Hood's division, had arrived at Gettysburg at 2:00 A.M. on July 2, after a twenty-four–hour march, and had taken up a position on the extreme Confederate right flank, opposite Round Top. There they waited until nearly four o'clock in the afternoon, while Brigadier General E. McIver Law's brigade pulled up on their right, before making an attack. The Texas Brigade was under constant bombardment from Union artillery on the hills above them.

on we moved. So soon as we cleared the brow of the hill and became exposed to the enemy's artillery, off we went, not at an orderly double-quick, but in a wild, frantic and desperate run, yelling, screaming and shouting; over ditches, up and down hill, bursting through garden fences and shrubbery, occasionally dodging the head as a bullet whistled by the ear. Arriving in a road, we halted a minute or two, reformed and started again. On we go with the same speed, jumping over and plunging through creeks, pulling through mud, struggling through underbrush, still keeping up the loud, irregular and terrible Confederate yell. Shells and grape shot, cannister and minnie balls, came hurtling through our ranks, bursting, screaming, whistling—still that same wild, reckless, unhesitating rush towards the enemy's guns.

Suddenly we find ourselves at the base of a range of hills—a rough, woody, rocky country. Here the great severity of the Federal Infantry stopped our progress, and then commenced a rapid, continuous and murderous musketry fight; we at the base, they on the sides and top of the hills. From behind trees and huge rocks we poured in our fiery discharges; the din was incessant and deafening. "Keep your eyes on the colors," would be occasionally shouted and repeated; "close to the right," "they are giving back," and other similar commands and exclamations could be heard during the short intervals of firing.

During this musketry engagement we were within from twenty-five to fifty yards of the enemy. The trees were literally barked, and thousands of bullets flew to atoms against the hard rocks. Our line was compelled finally to retire, and left me wounded in the hands of the enemy.

I tried to feign dead, but it would not answer, and some time after I was taken to the enemy's rear.

Thus ended as much as I know of the second day's fight.[4]

[4] When the attack finally got under way, Barziza's company fought across the valley, crossed the Emmetsburg Road, and worked their way

During the artillery fight above mentioned, I saw Gen. [Lieut. Gen. James] Longstreet [5] in a small wood immediately behind our batteries, sitting on his horse like an iron man with his spyglass to his eye, coolly watching the effect of our shots. Limbs of trees fell and crashed around him, yet he sat as unmoved as a statue. I really believe he loves the music of cannon-shot; if so, it is an affection that is not indulged in by his faithful soldiers.

Two days of terrible carnage had passed, and yet nothing decisive had been gained. The insatiable spirit of war had not been appeased, and blood again must flow. Oh, War! War! Who can realize all thy horrors, and who but a soldier can tell of the terrible doings of Battle? No pen can describe, no pencil can portray a battle field! As well hope to imitate the thunder's sound, or paint the fiery lightning; to mimic the roar of the

---

along the northern shoulder of Round Top to the deathtrap of Devil's Den, between the big hill and Little Round Top, to its north. It was in this area, where Confederate and Union infantrymen fought from rock to rock, firing at close range and often intermingling their confused lines, that Captain Barziza was wounded. Hood's attack from the right had stalled short of the hilltops. So had the Confederate attack all along the line, although at one point the Union line had been breached near the center, but hurriedly plugged; on the extreme left of the Confederate attack, a temporary foothold had been gained on Culp's Hill. Both sides had lost many men in the second day's fighting, but the Confederates could least afford their losses.

[5] Longstreet, commanding the Confederate First Army Corps at Gettysburg, of which Barziza's Company C of the Fourth Regiment, Texas Brigade, Hood's Division, was a part, has been described by his enemies as having maintained a strangely detached attitude throughout the Battle of Gettysburg. He was said to have opposed Lee's decision to force a decisive battle at this point, preferring to skirt the Union forces here and wait for a better showdown point nearer Washington. Longstreet was said to have stalled throughout most of July 2, after Lee had ordered him to attack early that morning, before finally starting his attack in the late afternoon. Such an excellent authority as Glenn Tucker (*High Tide at Gettysburg,* p. 217), however, says Longstreet obviously had no order to attack early in the day. Many modern historians, such as D. B. Sanger and K. P. Williams, agree.

tempest-tossed ocean, or put upon canvass the glittering stars in the firmament; to catch the tones of the hurricane, or pencil the many-hued rainbow.

No tongue can convey an adequate idea of the roar of cannon and the rattle of musketry—the cheering shout and hurried command—the tramp of horse and ominous rumble of artillery—the death-groan and parting shriek. No painting can portray the scenes of War—desolate homes and abandoned fields—homeless women and affrighted children; the Battle-field—the long lines of troops—the glittering arms—the eager, restless countenance—the steady march—the desperate onset—the flashes of fire—the dead soldier—the smoke-thick air—the trampled ground—the dismantled trees—the mangled limbs—the broken musket—the strong horse writhing in the throes of death—the streaming blood and matted hair—the death dew upon the brow of the dying soldier—the intensely, indescribably wild and thrilling aspect of strong men in the storm of Battle.

Abstractly, how positively foolish and senseless it seems for thousands of men to be engaged in deadly conflict with others, entire strangers to themselves, and, as the soldiers say, "nobody mad." In the morning, they will be in eager haste to take each other's lives; in the evening, the one kindly supporting and ministering to his wounded foe. A soldier's life tends to engender a feeling of indifference to future danger and an almost recklessness to the present. On his march, he is full of fun and humor, and sings his songs cheerily around his smoky camp fire—amuses himself in camp by often the most childish diversions—goes into ecstacies over a letter—shouts till his throat is sore at the waving of a white handkerchief, and jests with his comrade a minute before his own death.

A Battle is a terrible and fearful, but grand and magnificent display. How quiet and calm just before action! as though nature held its breath, and the very elements wait expectant upon the impending conflict. Men and cannon are moved into position quietly, deliberately and cautiously. Groups of Generals are col-

47

lected upon some commanding eminence. At a given signal the artillery begins to belch forth its horrid missiles. The air is filled with the bursting, screaming, hissing death-messengers. The roar is incessant. The very elements now appear to be at war, and all the thunderbolts of Heaven seem to be turned loose from the hands of an angry and destroying God. The tough trees, survivors of a thousand storms, are broken and dismantled; huge strong horses are felled in death like so many toys and playthings; whole ranks of living, moving men are mown down by the merciless shot and shell. Meantime, the supporting columns are ranged ready to advance, the men crouching down on the earth as they "lie under the shelling."

Half an hour upon an occasion like this seems an age; and the mind is so keenly tortured and oppressed by anxiety, that one feels as physically wearied, as if he had been on a long and tiresome march. The feelings that take possession of a soldier on the eve of advancing into a fight, can be known only to those who have experienced them. The heart is heavy; the blood feels as if it was congealed; the breath comes short and quick, and it is a relief to move on. As the Battle progresses, the sharp, desultory fire of the skirmishers startles every one into energy. The line presses forward and the engagement becomes general. Shells are bursting, shrapnel screaming, grapeshot whistling, and bullets fly thick as rain-drops. Men are cheering, cursing, raving—horses plunging and neighing wildly; then comes the deadly onset—the rush, the repulse, the victory!

The continued ring of musketry mingled with the louder reports of cannon, the long lines of burning flame, the dust, smoke, confusion and uproar, the sudden intervals of firing, only to recommence with redoubled fury, utterly defy conception, and seem as though ten thousand fiends were holding their infernal orgies.

Cold, heat, rain, fatigue and danger are alike disregarded, and even God himself is, for the time, forgotten. Borne along in this human current, the soldier steps over the body of his dead brother, and rushes on unheeding the imploring cries of his best friend. Men seem like devils who have wrested the instruments of wrath and destruction from the hands of the Almighty, and wield them for their mutual destruction.

And when the Battle is over, what a sight! Excitement allayed and passion subsided, the strong man becomes as a child, obedient, full of sympathy, kind, tender and obliging.

For miles the ground is strewn with the dead and dying—the wrecks of battle—the warm blood yet pouring from them; every ditch and ravine is filled with the poor mangled wretches, who have dragged themselves thither for shelter—friend and enemy bathing in the same water. And this is War! thousands of souls rush, unprepared, in the presence of their Maker; life is disregarded and men are made worse than the beasts of the field—all to satisfy the ambition, prejudice and fanaticism of individuals and communities.

How weary and care-worn the men look when they are drawn off from the carnage!

The roll is called and the list of casualties made out. And then the regrets and praises of the dead comrade are heard around the camp-fires; envy and animosity are forgotten and buried with him.

How lonely it makes one feel when, after a severe engagement, he misses scores of his comrades! It makes the heart sick to know that his place is forever vacated, his battles fought, his marches ended, his future fate mysterious, unknown, and, it may be, dreadful. Yet stern duty bids the survivors to forget, and soon, very soon, the same round of levity is renewed. But it is elsewhere that bitter, heart-rending grief reigns supreme. Parents, sisters and brothers, far away from the scene of contest, wait, oh, how anxiously! for tidings of the fight. Who can imagine with what overpowering anxiety a mother scans the list of casualties? And who can conceive of the pangs and oppression of that heart, when the name of her boy meets her eye "killed"? Then she thinks of him as a child, when, with infant faith, he bowed his little head upon her knee, and repeated the simple prayer she had taught him; when her heart bounded with pride and delight at the dawn of first intelligence; and she runs back over the scene of the gathering for the war, when, with fire in his young eye and the flush of courage upon his soft cheek, she beheld him attired as a soldier, and whispered her tearful prayer "God bless you." The grief-bowed father, too, in all the "silent manliness of grief," betrays the intense sorrow of the heart.

Now, alas! all their fond hopes, pride and anticipations are blasted. Away "upon the embattled plain," amid the clash of arms and the wild shouts of infuriated men, he breathed out his life on the bosom of his mother earth; no mother's hand supported the drooping head; no sister's voice cheered him in his dying hour; but, like a soldier he fought—a soldier he died.

Even his grave is unknown. No selected spot where affection can linger and bedew with tears; nay, he sleeps, it may be, in the same last bed with scores of his comrades, his ashes mingling with their own. And then the sable weeds of mourning; the haggard, care-worn countenance, faltering steps and gathering grey hairs, show too well the intense grief of the bereaved family.

Yet this is life; we go down to the grave—the sun shines as brightly, the birds sing as sweetly as before—the places that once knew us know us no more forever. Joy and revelry keep up the same revolving round, and a little while longer our places are refilled, oblivion sweeps over all traces of our former self, and we are not even missed by our nearest and dearest. Here, in this reflection, I am reminded of some beautiful lines by Miss Gould:

> "Alone I walked the ocean strand,
> A pearly shell was in my hand;
> I stooped and wrote upon the sand
> My name, the year, the day.
> As onward from the spot I passed,
> A lingering look behind I cast;
> A wave came rolling high and fast,
> And washed my lines away.

And thus me thought 'twill ever be
With every line on earth from me;
A wave of dark oblivion's sea
Will wash it from the place." [6]

But the horrors of war are seen and felt throughout the whole extent of the country in which it is waged. The fertile fields, just before blooming with rich verdure and golden grain, are now desolate; breastworks and rifle-pits are seen in the whole land, and the appearance is that of a vast camp-ground and burial place. That which was once all peaceful and flourishing is now a waste and a desert. The people themselves partake of the appearance of the country. Women, grown old in youth, are pale and full of distress; children, ill-clad, idle and almost abandoned. The whole land is filled with mourning and lamentation; scarcely a family but deplores the loss of a loved one. Thousands of hobbling, crippled creatures, remain as the sad evidences of war, left, it may be, upon the cold charities of a colder world; and, when the war shall be ended, their good deeds may even be forgotten, and they may wander forth friendless and in want, with perhaps the notice of the passers-by of "poor fellow, he lost his leg or arm at Gettysburg or Chicamauga." Yet, however terrible is war, it is a necessary evil. There is no other umpire between nations. Artillery and musketry must, and ever will settle extreme political difficulties. The price of liberty is not only "eternal vigilance," but oceans of red blood. To die a freeman, or to live a slave, is often the bitter alternative, and infamous is he who hesitates in the choice. The reward is greater than the sacrifice; and upon the dreadful ruin which war inaugurates and leaves behind, the Temple of Liberty is reared, fair, firm, proud, blood-cemented, and baptized in fire. The libations of blood only sanctify it the more, and make it the more worth preserving. Its altar will be the more

[6] He quotes the first two stanzas of "A Name in the Sand," from *The Diosma,* by Miss Hannah Flagg Gould (1789–1865), pp. 131–132.

sacred for the red stains with which it is covered, and liberty's pilgrims will kneel around its base, only regretting that their own blood had not smoked upon it.

The goal of independence is only to be reached by trying these horrors; let these sacrifices be made with willing hearts; pay in blood and suffering for the blessed boon, and a proud heritage will descend to the survivors.

Chapter Third.

The Rear of the Federal Army—The Battle
of the 3d of July—Field Hospital—Horrible
Scenes—Conversations with the Federals—
Their Views, &c.—Removal to Gettysburg—
The Confederate Hospital at Gettysburg—Fed-
eral Notions and Arguments.

N PASSING to the rear I saw the reinforcements of the
enemy coming up, and was indeed somewhat surprised at the *nonchalance* they exhibited in marching
steadily towards the firing.

I was taken to the Field Hospital of the Twelfth Army Corps,
which had been established some distance in the rear of the
lines. It consisted of the barn and other out-houses of a farm,
sheds, &c., besides a great quantity of hospital tents, which
were afterwards pitched.

About mid-day on Friday the battle of the 3d day opened
heavily; the artillery was terrific; as it progressed, great anxiety
was discernable among the Federals; the surgeons ceased their
operations and looked anxiously to the front; hospital flags were
perched on the fences, trees and houses; soon came streams of
ammunition wagons, ambulances and disabled artillery, driving
frantically to the rear; thousands of soldiers rushed back, and
were driven up again to the front by cavalry in their rear; the
wounded Federals, who were able to walk, were sent off hastily,
and the scene was that of a routed and panic-stricken army. We,

Confederates, who were at the hospital, were buoyant, and strained our eyes to see the grey backs rushing across the open field. But, alas! the storm gradually grew less violent, wavered, became more distant, and we knew the day was a bitter one for us.[1] A little more vigor on the part of the Confederates that day would have secured the victory. Whilst the fight was raging this day, I was so confident that I remarked to the surgeon of the 12th corps,[2] "Gen. Lee would have his Head Quarters by to-night ten miles on the Baltimore Pike." "It must be confessed," he replied, "that this looks somewhat like it." During all this day hundreds of wounded, both Confederate and Federal, were brought in.[3] Our wounded were generally well treated, and were put side by side with the enemy's. Every shelter in the neighborhood was crammed; even hay-lofts were filled with the bleeding, mangled bodies. The surgeons, with sleeves rolled up and bloody to the elbows, were continually employed in amputating limbs. The red, human blood ran in streams from under the operating tables, and huge piles of arms and legs, withered and horrible to behold, were mute evidences of the fierceness of the strife.

He who has never seen the rear of an army during and immediately after a battle, can form no idea of the scene, while the mere mention of a Field Hospital to a soldier, brings up

[1] The battle of the third day opened with a terrific cannonade from 125 Confederate guns concentrated on the Union center, starting around 1 P.M. and lasting for two hours, until the Confederate ammunition was nearly exhausted. This was followed by Pickett's spectacular drive into the Union center, which almost broke the Federal line, but failed for lack of support and ended in disaster.

[2] John McNulty, surgeon and medical director of the 12th Corps (*War of the Rebellion: Official Records of the Union and Confederate Armies,* Series 1, XXVII, 197).

[3] Thomas L. Livermore (*Numbers and Losses in the Civil War in America: 1861–65,* pp. 102–103) gives Confederate wounded at Gettysburg as 18,735, Union wounded 14,529. The losses on the second and third days were spectacular on both sides.

recollections of blood and brains, mangled limbs, protruding entrails, groans, shrieks and death. And when night comes upon them, and their wounds begin to grow chill, and pains shoot piercingly through them, then the deep and agonizing groans, the shrill death-shriek, the cries for water, opium, any thing, even death, make up the most horrible scene that can be conceived of. See that poor, bleeding boy turn his face to the surgeon and ask, "Doctor, is my wound mortal." And oh! what shades of agony, despair and dread flit across his features, as he hears the reply, "I fear it is, sir!" There lies one mortally wounded, sleeping "unto death," under the influence of opium, which has been given in large quantities to let him die easy. Now, one goes off in a convulsive spasm, another with a shriek, which causes the hair even of a hardened soldier to stand on end. And then the dead are laid out in long rows, with their naked faces turned up to the sun, their clothes stiff with the dried blood, and their features retaining in death the agony and pain which they died with; and presently they are dragged forth and thrust into a shallow pit, with, perhaps, the coarse jest of a vulgar soldier for their requiem, and bloody blankets for their winding sheets. What a blessing is it that the gentle and tender-loved ones at home are spared the sight of the last moments of their torn and mangled soldiers!

I could here but notice the exquisite order and arrangement of the Medical Department in the Federal army. Their ambulance corps is very numerous, and the supply of medicines is plentiful. Their surgeons assume a great deal of authority, and are feared and respected by the soldiers. Indeed, as might be expected from the material of their army, there is much distance kept up between officers and men; even their non-commissioned officers are ever mindful of the difference between themselves and the men.

I had opportunities for frequent conversation with the officers and soldiers, who seemed always eager for an argument. I was astonished to find what indifference prevailed amongst their soldiers in regard to the appointment and removal of their commanding Generals. Many of them did not know, nor did they seem to care who was in command of their army at this time. They all spoke well of Gen. Lee, and acknowledged him to be the "greatest Captain of the age." Many of them enquired whether it was true that Stonewall Jackson was really dead, or was it a story hatched up by their newspapers.[4] I heard several express the belief that had Jackson been present, we would have won the battle, "for," said they, "he would have gotten lost and turned up somewhere in our rear." On Saturday, the 4th, the wildest rumors were current. [Maj. Gen. George B.] McClellan was in Lee's rear with 150,000 militia, the Potomac had risen, Vicksburg had fallen, Charleston was ready to capitulate, and the Great Rebellion was crushed.[5] Their loud cheering resounded along their lines, and great joy prevailed amongst them.

It happened that it rained the day before, and I, with many others, was put in a hay loft, and, there being no other means of reaching the ground save a ladder, I couldn't come down for several days, a situation I am sure I had not much relish for. When, however, I was able to come down, I chanced to stop before a tent a moment, when some wounded Massachusetts officers who occupied it invited me in, and we became quite social; more especially so as they were provided with some good liquor and cigars. I called to see them daily, but will not say which more attracted me, their conversation or their cheer. I

[4] Jackson had died at Guiney's Station, Virginia, on May 10.

[5] On July 4 Lee pulled back his flanks, and in the evening started his retreat, the main force going through the mountains on the direct route to Williamsport, while a body convoying the immense train of wounded took the route by Chambersburg. It was true that the Potomac had risen. This caused Lee to concentrate his army in the vicinity of Williamsport, where he stayed until July 14. The great rebellion was not crushed, although the loss at Gettysburg was unquestionably the beginning of the end for Lee.

was surprised at their assertion that our army was much better disciplined than theirs, and that was all the balance they would confess in our favor. Like all New Englanders, they were bigoted and full of vanity; they pretended to think the Massachusetts men made better soldiers than any others, and indulged in unbecoming sneers against Pennsylvanians, because they had not turned out *en masse* for the defense of their State. They were full of argument, and would listen to nothing but the Union. True types of their agitating and vain-glorious fathers of Plymouth Rock memory. I would usually answer their arguments by assuring them that, as they had inaugurated War, we accepted the issue, and artillery and musketry must decide the quarrel.

Some of these Yankees are really patriotic, and honestly or at least fanatically so. I was standing near an old man when word was brought him that his son had fallen a few hours before; he received the news with some apparent grief, and replied with much earnestness, "I wish I had fifty to fall for the same cause." Oh, Liberty! how many crimes are committed in thy name!

It is but justice to say that the Chief Surgeon of the 12th Corps, Dr. McNulty, (I believe,) was very kind and attentive to our unfortunate people. This Field Hospital soon became very filthy, and the wounded were moved as fast as possible to Gettysburg. There was a college building in the town,[6] which had been used by the Confederates whilst they occupied the place. To this building most of the Confederates were carried. The rooms and passages were densely crowded, and wounds of every shape and description afforded subjects for the attention of the humanitarians. There was a handsome yard adjoining the building, interspersed with shade trees. Thousands of citizens from all parts of the North flocked to Gettysburg to see a battle field and get a view of the terrible rebels. New England preachers, indellibly and unmistakably stamped with the hypocritical sanctity of

[6] Pennsylvania College (Lutheran), now Gettysburg College.

57

Puritanism, stalked back and forth, with long faces and sanctimonious pretensions; they would occasionally come into a room and after sighing, and wheezing, and sucking their breath, would condescendingly give a poor rebel a tract and a cracker. Men and women, fresh from the very cess-pools of fanaticism and falsehood, would stand at the doors, and by their curious peering and simple questionings, gave much annoyance to our wounded. We always, however, had an infallible means at hand which would quickly cause their exodus, viz: we would ask them to give us money, clothing, or something to eat; we found this appeal to their charity would invariably rid us of their presence. But it is also just to state that many ladies showed much kindness to the "Rebels," but green Yankees never.

Whilst in Gettysburg, I could not but remark the difference between the conduct of our army and that of the enemy in invading our country. Here stood the town, after three days' hard fighting around and in it, almost entirely untouched. No wanton destruction of property of any description could be seen; no women and children complained that they were houseless and beggars. Then I called to mind the scenes around the city of Fredericsburg the winter previous; private houses sacked and burned, books, furniture, and every thing perishable utterly destroyed; women flying from burning houses with children in their arms, and insult and outrage at full license. I thought as I made the contrast in my own mind, of the utter uncongeniality of the two peoples, and thanked God that we were forever divided.

The Federals who came to visit us delighted to discuss the origin, cause and probable result of the Rebellion. Their chief arguments were of the most puerile character. For instance, they dwelt with much satisfaction upon the fact that we fired the first gun at Sumpter, whose reverberations echoed and re-echoed through the whole extent of the North, and aroused a people to arms. I have often had occasion since to remark that this origin of the war is in the mouth of every man, woman and child who holds that their cause is just. The politicians have made this a potent physic, and the rabble eagerly swallowed it, as it was plain and undeniable, and could be understood and discussed by all without any further study or investigation. Oh! that horrible gun which has brought about so much mischief! They contended that States bore relation to the Federal Government, analagous to that which Counties bore to the State Government; the absurdity of which is so plain to any man who does not wish to be wrong. They also contended with much spirit that the new States formed since the establishment of the Government were the property of the United States, as they had been bought and paid for by Federal money. Such, then, were the main pretexts among the masses of the people of that country, for persisting in this most unrighteous crusade against the lives and liberties of independent States. But when all else failed, when every specious pretense was met, they relied defiantly upon that most miserable and destructive delusion, "The Union must be preserved." They pretended to believe that the Southern people were led blindfolded by their leaders, and were held down by the iron rule of force. They admitted that our soldiers were brave and fought with reckless daring, that our Generals were of the first order; but they always referred with confidence to their superiority of numbers, consoling themselves with the everlasting reflection that three men can, in time, conquer one. They declared they would never cease to war until we acknowledged the supremacy of the "best Government the world ever saw." They insisted that if we still continued to resist them, that our only fate must, in the nature of things, be extermination, and on us be the sin of it.

Verily, this is a peculiar people. They believe the United States Government holds a magic wand with which it can sway the nations of the earth at pleasure. They are extremely bigoted, and actually bloated with self-love. They think everything of their's is better than anybody else's; their religion purer; their men braver, and women fairer; their country better; their manners and customs more enlightened, and their intelligence and culture immeasurably superior. Brim-full of hypocritical cant and Puritan ideas, they preach, pray and whine. The most parsimonious of wretches, they extol charity; the most inveterate blasphemers, they are the readiest exhorters; the worst of dastards, they are the most shameless boasters; the most selfish of men, they are the most blatant philanthropists; the blackest-hearted hypocrites, they are religious fanatics. They are agitators and schemers, braggarts and deceivers, swindlers and extortioners, and yet pretend to godliness, truth, purity, and humanity. The shibboleth of their faith is, "the Union must and shall be preserved," and they hold on to this with all the obstinacy peculiar to their nature. They say we are a benighted people, and are trying to pull down that which God himself built up.

Many of these bigots expressed great astonishment at finding that the majority of our men could read and write; they have actually been educated to regard the Southern people as grossly illiterate, and as little better than savages. The whole nation lives, breathes and prospers in delusion; and their chiefs control the springs of the social and political machine with masterly hands.

I could but conclude that the Northern people were bent upon the destruction of the South. All appeared to deprecate the war, but were unwilling to listen to a separation of the old Union. They justified the acts of usurpation on the part of their Government, and seemed submissive to the tyranny of its acts on the plea of military necessity; they say the Union is better than the Constitution, and bow their necks to the yoke in the hope of success against us. A great many, I believe, act from honest and conscientious principle; many from fear and favor; but the large majority entertain a deep-seated hatred, envy and jealousy towards the Southern people and their institutions.

They know (yet they pretend not to believe it) that Southern men and women are their superiors in everything relating to bravery, honesty, virtue and refinement; and they have become more convinced of this since the present war; consequently, their worst passions have become aroused, and they give way to frenzy and fanaticism.

We must not deceive ourselves; they are bent upon our destruction, and differ mainly in the means of accomplishing this end.

However much as sections and parties they hate each other, yet, as a whole, they hate us more.

They are so entirely incongruous to our people, that they and their descendants will ever be our natural enemies.

But this digression, concerning the Yankee people, has carried me too far from the main subject of this work.

Some days elapsed before supplies sufficient for the wounded could be collected at Gettysburg. The whole hospital building and grounds soon became impregnated with the peculiar and sickening odor of blood and wounds.

We amused ourselves by rummaging over some books and papers that lay scattered about the rooms.

Soon, however, many ladies from Baltimore came to visit us, and spoke words of good cheer and encouragement.

I shall ever remember a gentleman from Baltimore, who came into the room where I was, and left me a bottle of fine brandy; it was a glorious treat, and right heartily was it enjoyed.

The wounded were removed as fast as possible from Gettysburg to Baltimore. Accordingly, some two hundred were put in box cars, on straw, and started.

Whilst at the depot we, of course, had many words with the citizens.

Whilst passing through the street, a Federal soldier ran up to our column and said, "Boys, if those fellows (meaning the guards) treat you badly, you must not think any thing of it, as they never smelt gun-powder."

At the depot a citizen was declaiming severely against the wicked rebellion, and predicting grand results from Federal arms, when one of our ragged soldiers placed his hand on his shoulder, and the following colloquy ensued:

Rebel. "Mister, do you belong to the army?"

Yank. "No sir, I do not—my cousin does."

Reb. "Mister, did you ever belong to the army?"

Yank. "No sir; why?"

Reb. "Because, Mister, when a man in my country talks as big as you do, he generally has on soldier's clothes, and a cartridge box belted around him. I would advise you to put on harness and trot to Gen. [Maj. Gen. George G.] Meade [Army of the Potomac]."

Yank. "Oh! you needn't give yourself any concern about Meade—he isn't sick; when it becomes necessary for me to go in the army, I am ready to go."

Reb. "Yes, I see you going. I'll bet a treat for the crowd you have just paid the three hundred dollar commutation. Your style don't like bullets; and a cock shouldn't crow if he is afraid to fight."

Yank. "You are very assuming, sir, for a man who is now dependent on us and our people for your very existence, and who is well taken care of by those you come to destroy. You have no rights, sir, save what the clemency of your enemies, for humanity sake, grants you."

Reb. (*Somewhat piqued.*) "I will let you know, sir, that I feel myself under no obligations to your Government for my good treatment. Whatever humanity may be shown us is forced from your Government. I am a soldier of the Confederate States, and my Government is able to demand proper treatment for its soldiers. We have plenty of Yankees down South, and it is this, and not humanity, which makes your Government clement, and deters you from putting in practice your declared outlawry against rebels.[7]

[7] According to Mr. Morton Brown, 106 East 18th Street, Austin, his father, the late William Morton Brown, first lieutenant, Rockbridge

The Yankee was about to reply, but was stopped by the guard. He went off shaking his head, and muttering something about the "confounded rebels."

After traveling all night, we arrived in Baltimore at daybreak.

Ladies and children in numbers came crowding around the cars with refreshments, but were roughly and insultingly driven off by the guard.

For some reason we were compelled to lie in the cars all day until late in the evening.

Being provoked by the continued attempts of the ladies and boys to give us food and water, the officer of the guard had the hatches of the cars closed. Here, then, in a small box lay thirty helpless, bleeding men—their wounds very offensive and painful—almost suffocated, without a ray of light, and scarcely enough air to breathe. This piece of cruelty was continued for over half an hour, and when the hatches were again opened, we begged the ladies to go off, as they would kill us by this untold and wanton barbarity.

Crowds of men, women and children followed us towards the hospital.

We were in a sorry plight; our wounds had not been dressed for forty-eight hours; our clothes had never been changed since the battle—thus, bloody, dirty, ragged, bare-footed, bare-headed, and crippled, we marched through the streets of the monumental city, a spectacle of fiendish delight to some, but one of pity and sympathy to thousands of true subjugated Southerners, who inhabit this city.

Artillery, Army of Northern Virginia, C.S.A., who was a prisoner at Johnson's Island from 1863 to 1865, said one of the favorite songs of the Rebel prisoners included this stanza:

> While we starve here in frost and snow
> It is consoling for us to know
> That retaliation will be given
> Upon the Yanks in Libby Prison.

Everything in the city of Baltimore gave evidence of the presence of oppression and tyranny. A Federal flag streamed from almost every window, and little miniature ones stuck upon the breasts of hundreds, as if they were worn as a talisman against insult and outrage. If a little girl dared wave her handkerchief at the Confederates, she was arrested or maltreated by the armed minions of despotism. Ladies, with baskets of provisions, followed tremblingly on the side-walks, and would be shaken roughly by the arm and insulted, if they approached us. Sympathy and pity shone upon the features of hundreds; and the sly look and troubled countenance showed plainly how they had been taught to fear the arms of their own Government. Baltimore is literally crushed and broken by high handed tyranny; the petty, ill-bred plebeians, with shoulder-straps on, actually lord it over these unfortunate people, with all the mean oppression which characterizes men of low estate who have been suddenly elevated to power. I saw at the West Building Hospital a lady arrested by a lubberly, bloated, and uncouth Hospital Steward, because she gave a white handkerchief to a wounded Confederate. Similar instances of mean and pitiful exhibitions of power are of daily occurrence. What a commentary upon the boasted freedom of the United States! May the proud Southern race disappear from the earth before they call these people masters!

Hundreds of our wounded were here collected, and distributed to other places; some to David's Island, New York; others to Chester, Pennsylvania, and others to the various forts and prisons.

The Federals at this time were exceedingly jubilant. And, it must be confessed, that gloom was with the Confederates. Yet they were ever manly, impudent and independent.

From Baltimore I, with many others, was started on the cars for the hospital at Chester, Pennsylvania.

Chapter Fourth.

From Baltimore to Chester—Hospital at Chester—Visits and Attention of Ladies—Character of the Federal Soldiers—Their Women—Confederate Fast Day—Northern Democrats—Brutality of the Yankees in regard to our Dead—Departure for Johnson's Island.

HE TRIP from Baltimore to Chester was made without anything of special interest transpiring.

In traveling through the North, I was struck at the seeming state of prosperity of every class of industry. The laboring classes seemed to have plenty of employment, and received good wages; the merchants sold more goods apparently than ever; and it really did seem as though the war had given an impetus to every species of employment. No one would have supposed that this people was engaged in a most stupendous and exhausting war, had he not been so constantly reminded of it by gay uniforms, the display of banners, and martial music.

I could but feel, however, some gratification in the reflection, that all this was hollow and superficial, and that when the reaction did come it would be terribly retributive.

Everybody had plenty of money; and the currency was almost on a par with specie. Alas! what a difference has taken place in one short year! [1]

[1] In 1863 the North enjoyed comparative prosperity, with industries booming and the beginnings of inflation based on the issuance of gov-

Arriving at Chester, the "rebels" were a source of much curiosity to the inhabitants who had not seen many.

The town of Chester is situated on the railroad, about twelve miles from Philadelphia, contains, perhaps, two or three thousand souls, and is a very pretty and pleasant village.

The Confederate Hospital was about three-fourths of a mile out of the town, and comprised a college building [2] and several long, low-built wards. The college building was assigned to the officers. Besides these, there was a large number of comfortable hospital tents. The situation was indeed a pleasant and beautiful one, being upon a hill overlooking the town, with a neat and shady ground around, and two streams of water running near.

There were in all about fifteen hundred Confederates. The surgeons and attendants were in the main attentive, obliging and kind. The wards and beds were kept scrupulously clean and neat, and the whole place had an air of comfort, well calculated to work improvement in the condition of sick and wounded men.

There was a battalion on duty here, and dress parade was the order of every afternoon, when a brass band would regale us with national and sentimental airs, and sometimes with "Dixie." I have often remarked that this great Southern air is much of a favorite with the Federals. We were allowed a great many privileges at this place. Visitors were permitted to see us, and were allowed to distribute clothing amongst the needy. Thousands of grateful hearts all over the Confederacy will hold in

---

ernment notes, or greenbacks. By the summer of 1864 inflation had caught up with them. The U.S. bank note had dropped to a gold value of thirty-nine cents. Prices had practically doubled over those of 1860, but wages had risen only about 25 per cent. Farm prices had also lagged. Discontent, labor disputes, and some hardships were prevalent (Ernest Ludlow Bogart, *Economic History of the American People,* pp. 676–678).

[2] Pennsylvania Military College.

THE · ADVENTURES

OF A

PRISONER OF WAR;

AND

LIFE AND SCENES IN

FEDERAL PRISONS:

JOHNSON'S ISLAND, FORT DELAWARE, AND POINT
LOOKOUT;

BY

AN ESCAPED PRISONER

OF HOOD'S TEXAS BRIGADE.

———◆◆◆◆———

HOUSTON, TEXAS :
RICHARDSON & OWEN'S PRINTING ESTABLISHMENT.

1865

Title page of the original journal published
in 1865.

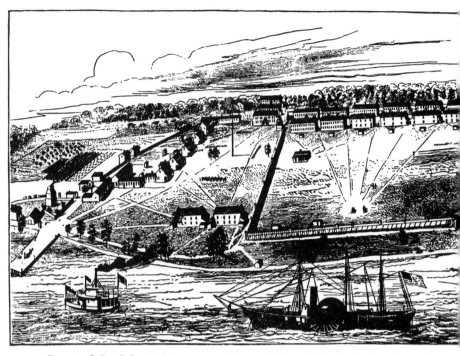

Depot of Confederate Prisoners on Johnson's Island, Sandusky Bay, Lake Erie.

From a lithograph of a War-time sketch made by Edward Gould, Co. B., 128th Ohio. In the foreground is the U.S. steamer *Michigan*. The long radiating lines in the enclosure are paths leading from the prison blocks to the pumps. (Ed.—This caption accompanied the illustration in the *Publications of the Buffalo* [N.Y.] *Historical Society* [1906].)

fond remembrance the numerous acts of kindnesses they received from those noble females who watched, nursed and provided for our wounded soldiers.

Far away from their homes, stretched upon beds of pain and suffering, our heroic defenders here found new mothers and sisters; females devoted to the gallant men who upheld right against wrong.

I shall call no names, but their names are as "household words" in thousands of families from Virginia to Texas, and their labors and trials, amidst so many difficulties, will be remembered long after this war shall have ended. Many a mother's blessing has been invoked upon their heads, and many a sister's prayer has ascended in grateful remembrance of them.

Surely the women have been of more avail in this contest than thousands of armed men. They never grow despondent at defeat; they never murmur at privations and trials; they never talk of "giving up the ship."

But all over the land their efforts are unceasing, and prayers untiring for the support and aid of the weak against the strong. Thousands of devoted women in the North are looking on this struggle with anxiety and hope, and prayers for the success of our cause. May the choicest blessings come upon them and theirs. But even here, at the hospital, as everywhere else, could be seen that slavish fear of the Government, which obtains among them all. Abraham Lincoln ruled absolutely by inspiring his people with dread of his power. The surgeons, and others in position, were continually in trepidation, lest the leniency shown us should provoke the resentment of their masters at Washington. They were constantly uneasy, lest some paid Government spy should report them as "suspicious persons." Thus had these people been reduced to the condition of abject serfs, and instead of holding affection for their Government, regarded it as an immense engine of punishment, and their main care and actions were devoted to the means of keeping out of its way.

Whilst we were here, the day set apart by President Davis for fasting and prayer came around.[3] The following reminder was circulated secretly throughout all the wards:

"Next Friday, the 21st of August, being the day recommended by President Davis for fasting and prayer by the people of the Confederate States, it is proposed and earnestly desired that the officers and soldiers of the Confederate army, in this hospital, do observe that day by abstaining from breakfast on that morning; thus exhibiting unceasing devotion to that cause for which we have periled our lives and fortunes, and in patriotic respect for the proclamation of our President."

This day was thus kept, and hundreds respected, for the first time, such a proclamation, and then while in the enemy's country, and prisoners of war. Thus do our noble soldiers, in whatever condition they may be placed, still hold fast to their hopes and dearest principles, and utter defiance to their enemies.

During my stay here, I must confess that I became actually disgusted with profanity and vulgarity. The Federal soldiers continually and on all occasions indulged in the most blasphemous oaths, such as even caused a chill to run over any common swearer; while their obscene language was absolutely revolting to the ear. I also remarked what little respect they had for females of their own class, who came every afternoon to witness the parade. They indulged in profanity and even vulgarity in their presence as freely as if they had been in the guard-room; and their frequent hints and lascivious expressions showed too plainly how lightly they esteemed the virtue of their women.

I have often had occasion to remark the difference in the estimation of the men North and South for their women. They do not hold that high regard and true esteem for womanly virtue

[3] In a proclamation issued July 21, 1863, President Jefferson Davis called upon the people of the Confederacy to observe August 21 as "a day of fasting, humiliation and prayer." This was one of the ten such proclamations issued by Davis during the war (James D. Richardson [ed.], *Messages and Papers of the Confederacy,* I, 328).

that characterize the chivalrous Southerners. And this habit increasing in disregard as it descends in caste, it will be found that the masses of laboring people have carried it to such an extent as to amount almost to prostitution.

What more can be expected of a people who preach and practice free-loveism—only another name for public and licensed debauchery!

During our stay at Chester we had occasion to see and converse with a great many Northern Democrats, as they were then called. They expressed much admiration for the bravery and perseverance of the Southern people, and all evinced a desire to treat with us peacefully in view of a restoration of the "Union as it was." They denounced the Administration in the strongest terms, and opposed totally its policy. But they seemed unwilling to believe that we were really determined upon absolute separation. They declared that they did not desire, nor would they ever interfere with slavery or any other of our local institutions; that they held us in great respect as a people, and regarded us members of the same great political family; that they knew we had been driven to extremities by the present policy of their Government; that the abolition leaders on the one side, and the disunion leaders on the other, had brought about all this mischief; that it only required a spirit of fairness and conciliation to bring us all back to our former allegiance, and that their every effort was directed to this end.

They expressed astonishment and disbelief when we told them that separation, absolute and forever, was the determination of our people; that we would reject at all times all overtures for peace, save the recognition of our independence; that we wished, and would accept no offers, promises, or guarantees, only on the condition of becoming independent States.

They would not be convinced that this was a true representation of the great masses of our people; they replied, however, that, if this were really true, and the Northern people and democrats knew of this all-pervading feeling in the Southern

69

mind, "where there is now," said they, "one soldier in the army, there would then be *ten*."

We insisted that they should not deceive themselves; that we were prepared for the worst, and should resolutely meet all in arms, whether they be republicans or democrats; that we could not regard them as our friends any more than the opposite party; that they would first attempt by policy and persuasion to accomplish that which the dominant party sought to do by arms, and that, according to their own admissions, we would eventually be forced to resort to war. In fact, I then regarded the democratic party at the North as properly an opposition party, and not as a peace party, except upon the terms of reconstruction.

And truly it was better for our people that they were not in power, lest by continued overtures of conciliation, by fair promises of constitutional guarantees and the like policy, perhaps by strategy and fraud, they might in all probability have succeeded in quenching the fires of enthusiasm amongst us on the one hand, and appealing to our fears and interest on the other, until there would have risen in our midst a reconstruction party, which calamity would have been "the beginning of the end," and our chains would soon have been more firmly riveted. It may be very true that many of this democratic party might have been at heart willing to have seen the independence of the South, and unwilling to have entered into a war for the purpose of coercion, but through policy might have kept their real sentiments hidden until the proper time came for their avowal. I had no doubt but there were thousands of this character; but I do not believe they *then* represented the sentiments of the masses of that party, whatever the same party may *now* be.

But in a republican government there are various and imperative causes for strong partisan opposition. Every party is ambitious of power, and adherents are brought over and maintained by various pretexts; by promises to some, and rewards to others. Disappointment and baffled ambition add many to the ranks of an opposition. For instance, General McClellan did not array himself against the Administration until he was deprived of command;[4] yet, being deposed, he strongly endorsed the democratic candidate, [Judge George W.] Woodward, for Governor of Pennsylvania, who was a bitter and unsparing enemy of the republicans.[5] In fact they who avowed themselves for peace, did so because they regarded it as the shortest and surest way to the reconstruction of the Union, not that they thought we were right and they were wrong.

The desire for power and influence is so strong and influential an incentive, that we need not go beyond this to account for the intense hostility of the democrats to the Administration. The truth is that they all affect a fanatical glorification for the "old flag," and cry out "Union." And the Southern people would have been much wiser and better off at the outset, if they had made up their minds that neither foreign intervention nor Northern sympathy would ever aid them in their struggle for independence, but upon their own strong arms and stout hearts depended entirely their success. Resistance, fierce and bloody, has been and ever will be the means of a nation's regeneration from vassalage; and he who lulls himself into inactivity in these vain hopes, will find too late that national and political sympathy and aid are the offsprings of policy and interest. In this world the strong are ever willing to help the strong; the rich make the rich richer; and with this feeling of self-interest so intimately blended with our individual selves, we may expect it to be the chief spring of action amongst nations. There is one other power, however, when it takes possession of the breast, displaces all others, and that is *fanaticism;* it raised a Cromwell

[4] President Lincoln's General Order 182, issued November 5, 1862, relieving McClellan from command, was received by McClellan November 7 (Kenneth P. Williams, *Lincoln Finds a General,* II, 475).

[5] In the Pennsylvania gubernatorial election of 1863, Governor Andrew Gregg Curtin, incumbent, Republican, was opposed by Democrat Judge Woodward in a vigorous campaign (W. F. Dunaway, *History of Pennsylvania,* p. 428).

and deluged a kingdom in blood; it erected the guillotine and was made drunk with gore; it pervaded the Northern mind and brought forth war, and is now reveling in a bloody carnival. Time was when we wished no harm to these Northern people; when all we asked was non-interference with us; their future prosperity and glory would not even have been displeasing to us. But for more than three years we have been the objects of their persecution and resentment. They have at last extinguished every feeling of friendship; they have provoked our entire population to desperation; every tie is forever severed, and they have succeeded in turning us into mortal and irreconcilable foes. There will be no need to make the Southern boy, like Hannibal, swear eternal enmity to the Yankee race. The blood of their murdered fathers, and the tears of their outraged mothers, will call aloud for vengeance; and whether in our own national armies or in the ranks of foreigners, defending our own homes or carrying the fires of war in their midst, coming years will yet witness the fruits of the seed they have sown. Hereafter their honor will be our shame, their prosperity our loss, and in every condition of life, generations yet to come will keep alive those fires of hate they have taken so much pains to kindle. If we must eventually fall, let us pull down that country and that people in the general wreck. If ruin must come, let it be universal as regards that nation—loyalist and rebel, friend and foe, "in one red burial blent." Better, far better sell ourselves to foreign despots, than be conquered provinces of this people. Let us welcome the bonds of French Empire, or the chains of the Russian Autocrat, rather than bow our necks to the bigoted descendants of the Puritans. If we fall, America shall fall with us, and rivers of blood shall smoke upon the red altar of Mars. Let no people have a name and existence who shall stand up and call themselves our conquerors. And when the worst comes to the worst, welcome destruction, so our foe be strangled in our death-grapple!

But to my narrative. During my stay at Chester the Chaplain

held divine services every Sunday. He was an Episcopalian; but, in offering prayer in the presence of the Confederates, I am pleased to say that he had sufficient respect for our feelings as to omit the invocation upon the President of the United States.[6]

The Confederate officers were not allowed to visit the wards of the privates; but under the excuse of going to the bath-rooms, which were in those wards, they managed to have mutual intercourse often.

Very few accepted the oath,[7] so far as I know of, or could learn.

I was shocked at the brutality of the Yankee soldiers, who were stationed here, in their treatment of our dead. There was a "dead-house," of course, connected with the hospital, and they took the bodies out daily. A great many of our dead were examined, *post mortem,* by the surgeons. I have often stood by and seen the men put them in the coffins; they would drag them by the feet and hair, and indulge in all sorts of vulgar and unseemly expressions and witticisms. When they came to one who had been examined, *post mortem,* they would put the hands on his naked breast, and exclaim, "Hello! here's another one that they've gutted." Such was the treatment our noble and heroic dead would receive from their foes in arms. Verily, the jackal can safely kick the dead lion!

In the latter part of August a party of us bid farewell to Chester, and started for Johnson's Island. We traveled through Philadelphia, Harrisburg, Pittsburg, Mansfield, to Sandusky city [Ohio].

[6] A "Prayer for the President of the United States and Others in Authority" is customarily used in the Orders of Morning and Evening Prayer in Episcopal services. See *Book of Common Prayer,* Protestant Episcopal Church in the United States.

[7] Prisoners taking either the Oath of Allegiance or the Oath of Obligation Not To Bear Arms could be released and taken through the lines under a flag of truce (*War of the Rebellion: Official Records,* Series 2, III, 52).

On arriving at the latter place we were honored by a great turn out of men, women and children. About twenty kettle-drums, beat by little boys, and fifes and flags in profusion, attested the jubilation of the conquerers. In an hour or less we took the steamer, and were soon on our way to that far-famed Federal prison.

Chapter Fifth.

Johnson's Island and the Prison—Life in Prison
—Rations—Water—The Hoffman Battalion—
Sutler—The Canada Expedition—Long and te-
dious Winter Nights—Amusements—Debating
Societies—Dramatic Performances—Poetical ef-
fusions by the Prisoners.

N THE 4TH September I was ushered in the prison
yard through the "small gate."

Johnson's Island, so called from the name of its
owner, is a small island about a mile and a half
long, and about four or five hundred yards wide. It is situated
about three miles from the main-land, opposite Sandusky city,
Ohio. Opposite the north side of the island a peninsula extends
eastwardly, and is about three-fourths of a mile or a mile from
the island. North-easterly the island extends to Lake Erie; part
of this small island is washed by Sandusky bay, and part by the
lake. The nature of the ground is rolling, or rather gradually
inclined towards the shore.

A fine view is afforded by the bay and lake, which latter
stretches out beyond the sight.

The prison consists of an enclosure made of thick plank,
about fourteen feet in height, on the top and outside of which
there is a platform around the whole for the walks of the
sentinels.

The "pen" encloses, I believe, about eight acres, much of

which is taken up by the buildings. There are thirteen blocks, or separate hastily constructed buildings, numbered from one to thirteen inclusively. When the buildings were first constructed,[1] four of these blocks were reserved for officers, and the rest designed for privates. But as it is now and was then used solely for officers, they occupy all the blocks.

The four blocks above were somewhat more desirable residences than the rest, being divided into small rooms about twelve by fourteen, and designed to accommodate twelve men. The other blocks consisted of three rooms up-stairs, each room accommodating about fifty men. The bunks were ranged on all sides, three tiers high, each bunk to accommodate two men. One stove was allowed, and some benches. The lower story of these blocks had two little rooms, one at each end, with a cooking stove in each, between which rooms one long hall extended, used for eating, and also for sleeping. Each block was, for convenience, divided into two messes—No. 1 and 2; each mess usually numbered about one hundred and forty men, who did their cooking in one stove, about two feet and a half or three feet square. Each mess was again sub-divided, at pleasure, into smaller ones. There was a "head" of each main mess—one of our own men—appointed by a Yankee corporal, whose duty it was to call the roll or assist in it, and to receive the rations, and who otherwise acted as a "go-between" for the corporal and ourselves.

I neglected to mention that we were required to deposit all money, both Federal and Confederate, outside with the authorities.

The blocks were arranged in two rows, with a broad street between them. We were permitted to walk in this street, and also behind the rows of blocks, inside a series of stakes, which limited nearer approach to the walls. On the lake side these stakes were ranged from forty to fifty yards from the wall, and

[1] October, 1861.

between were two small houses for condemned men, and which, of course, we were not permitted to visit. Of the character of these cells, and the condition of the inmates, I shall have something to say hereafter.

Outside the "bull-pen," (as our prison-yard was universally termed,) were the barracks for the guards, and the houses and families of the officers in command and on duty there.

We were allowed the privilege of the yard from reveille until retreat; when retreat sounded, about sun-set, all were required to keep within their rooms until the next morning.

Every morning each mess answered to roll-call, under the superintendence of a Yankee corporal. If any one was absent, his rations were taken away, and he put upon extra duty, or otherwise punished, unless he gave sufficient excuse to the corporal.

We usually drew a week's rations at a time of everything except bread, which was issued every day. Our rations were very scanty, and those who were so unfortunate as not to have friends and acquaintances in the North, often went to bed hungry. They pretended to issue us meat, sugar, coffee, rice, hominy, or peas, and candles; but this long array was only for appearance sake; for instance, one man would draw a piece of candle about two inches long for ten days. The hominy or rice they occasionally gave us was almost invariably musty and half-spoilt, while the apology for coffee was very unwholesome.

We had all the work about the place to do—cook, wash, scour, dig pits and ditches, and load the truck carts. The cooking stoves were always crowded, inside and out, as may be imagined, when one small stove was allowed one hundred and forty or fifty men.

Two pumps, with pipes extending to the bay, furnished us with water. But early in the winter these pipes became choked with ice, and rendered the pumps useless. Two holes, about eight feet deep, were then dug in the yard, and pumps put in them, and these afforded the only sources of water for more than twenty-five hundred men. I have many a time been actually and painfully thirsty, and yet in sight of an ocean of fresh water.

As soon as reveille sounded, crowds would collect around the pumps with buckets, canteens, &c., and in an hour the wells would be exhausted. I have seen scores of men standing in two ranks by these pumps for hours, exposed to rain, snow, sleet and wind, waiting for the water to rise at the rate of about a green bucket full in half an hour.

And this state of things continued throughout almost the entire winter, until Gen. [Brig. Gen. H. D.] Terry relieved Col. Pierson of the command. Gen. Terry permitted us to go the Bay, under guard, and supply ourselves.

The Hoffman Battalion [Inf., Ohio], under command of Lieutenant-Colonel Wm. S. Pierson, constituted our guards during the summer, until reinforcements were sent them, in anticipation of an uprising.

This battalion comprised as graceless, impudent and insulting a set of ruffians as was ever gotten together. The sentinels availed themselves, with few exceptions, of every occasion to insult us and shoot. They had never seen service, and were very valiant towards unarmed men.

These scoundrels often fired at our prisoners without the slightest pretext, and took great delight in ordering a "damned rebel" to do so and so. The petty lieutenants too would sometimes promenade the yard, and assume the most ridiculous airs and attitudes, much to the disgust of the prisoners.

This battalion was afterwards filled up to a full regiment, and called the 128th Ohio; and if, as it is hoped, this regiment should ever take the field, the prisoners who have been under their control will take much delight in remembering Johnson's Island, and they will most certainly be handled with "gloves off."

Until the Canada alarm, we had a sutler in the yard, who issued paste-board checks for the money we had outside, and with these checks we were allowed to buy from him. We were then enabled to get any necessary article, either of food or clothing, if we had the funds; but we were soon deprived of this great convenience, a circumstance that must have been regretted more by the sutler than by ourselves, as he was making any quantity of money, and made such charges as he pleased.

Towards the latter part of the Fall, the inhabitants of the island were thrown into a fever of excitement, on account of a reported expedition to be fitted out from Canada, in order to release us. We could, at this time, easily have overcome our guards and captured the garrison, there being only about four or five hundred men guarding upwards of twenty-five hundred. To guard against an uprising, there were two block-houses, with small howitzers, to sweep the yard, and loop-holes for riflemen; but these would not have been much in our way, had we determined on breaking out.

But we knew that we had no means of getting off the island after we had captured it.

However, this Canada expedition was to have come in the bay, and captured the gun-boat Michigan, which lay off the Island; and, on the appearance of the friendly vessels, the prisoners were to have risen against the garrison.[2] It would

[2] In August, 1863, Secretaries J. A. Seddon (of War) and S. R. Mallory (of Navy) suggested to Lieutenant R. D. Minor of the Confederate navy an enterprise having as its main purpose the release of the prisoners on Johnson's Island. The Confederate government furnished $110,000 and a party of twenty-two naval officers. Minor and B. P. Loyall reached Montreal on October 21. They established communication with the prisoners through the personal columns of the *New York Herald*, in which it was announced that a "carriage will be at the door a few nights after the 4th of November."

The final plan was that the party, posing as mechanics and laborers bound for Chicago to be employed on the waterworks there, and now numbering fifty-four, with the addition of escaped prisoners found in Canada, would book passage on one of a line of steamers running from Ogdensburg to Chicago. They would seize the steamer, arrive at John-

have been a great achievement had it been carried out; the gun-boat above was the only armed vessel of the United States on the lake, according to a treaty with Great Britain. With this boat in our possession or destroyed, we could have ravaged every town and city on the lake shore. However, the expedition, in point, failed; the object of it is said to have been betrayed by a Canadian [3] who had enlisted in it, and who communicated it to the Governor-General of Canada,[4] who informed Lord Lyons [5] at Washington.

The object and time of the expedition were known in the prison; it was not generally known, however, before-hand, because the Yankees always kept spies in the prison, who passed themselves off for Confederates, and thus they generally found out any contemplated movement which was publicly canvassed amongst us. How we gained our information of this raid on the lake is a matter that does not pertain to this narrative.

The Yankees were greatly alarmed; they ordered off the sutler, stopped the mails and express, dug rifle-pits lake-ward, planted artillery, fortified Cedar Point, which commands the entrance to the bay, and received a whole regiment of reinforcements,

---

son's Island at daylight, take the *Michigan* by surprise, turn her guns on the prison headquarters, and demand the surrender of the island. Frederick J. Shepard, "The Johnson's Island Plot, An Historical Narrative of the Conspiracy of the Confederates, in 1864, To Capture the U.S. Steamship Michigan on Lake Erie, and Release the Prisoners of War in Sandusky Bay," *Publications of the Buffalo Historical Society,* IX (1906), 1–51.

[3] McCuaig (*ibid.,* p. 19). Another source, Robin W. Winks' *Canada and the United States: The Civil War Years* (p. 149), indicates that the plot was exposed by the British consul at Baltimore.

[4] Viscount Charles Stanly Monck.

[5] Richard B. P. Lyons, British minister in Washington. A late night telegram to Lyons authorized the minister to warn U.S. Secretary of State Seward of "a serious and mischievous plot" that had been originated in the Canadas by unidentified people who were "hostile to the United States" (Winks, *Canada and the United States,* p. 148).

which kept increasing, until Gen. Terry's brigade from the Army of the Potomac swelled the number to some six or seven thousand. The sentinels became doubly vigilant, and many of our privileges were curtailed.

I remember an amusing incident connected with this excitement. One still, calm, dark night, about twelve o'clock or after, a mischievous fellow stepped out on the steps of his block and crowed three times like a shanghai; scarcely had the echo died away, when it was answered in the same manner from the other end of the yard. Immediately the long roll beat to arms, and the Yankees were formed, waiting for the attack, whilst those of the rebels, who were awake, laughed at their scare, and quietly kept between their blankets.

He who has been in confinement knows that the longer he remains so, the more irksome it becomes. One becomes perfectly miserable; the mind cannot be fixed upon the same subject any length of time; restlessness, anxiety and dejection fill the breast, and one becomes almost cowered.

I think, and hundreds will agree with me, that the most heavy and lonely hours I ever passed, were during the winter nights in prison. The yard was one vast mud-hole, knee-deep, and consequently we could take little or no exercise; at half past eight or nine, the drum beat for lights to be put out. In the dark, around a smouldering fire, some of the most restless ones would sit and talk, and smoke, and chew, and, lamenting their hard lot, watch the creeping hours as they would be called out by the sentinels. Visions of home and loved ones, of comfort, liberty, and plenty, would crowd into the bosom, and oppress the sad captive. Many a time have I, with others, sat up, hour after hour, thus in the dark, and longed for the morning to come.

Often we would amuse ourselves, at these times, by telling anecdotes, and such, too, as would not have fallen pleasantly on delicate ears. At these anecdotes we would, like a set of schoolboys, laugh immoderately, each one amused at the childishness of the other. This disturbance finally became such a nuisance, and prevented so many from sleeping, that we put a stop to it by a means which was both effectual and pleasing. This was the organization of a Court for the trial of offences committed there by any of these men. It is astonishing to see how childish grown-up men will become under these circumstances; they seek anything literally to "kill time," and as much interest was manifested in this Court as if it had been a Mayor's Court in a city.

Col. ——— was the Judge of this Honorable Court; Captains ——— and ——— the Prosecuting Attornies, Capt. ——— Sheriff, Lieut. ——— Deputy, and Lieut. ——— Clerk. There were some twelve or fourteen lawyers in the room, who were liberally patronized.

His Honor assumed as much dignity as if he had the judicial ermine about him; the senior Prosecuting Attorney, an able lawyer, stated, with great gravity, that he charged A or B with "talking after taps," "washing in the room," or "failing to do duty as detail;" "all this against the peace and dignity of this room." The sheriffs bustled about, and in loud voices ordered "silence," and "hats off gentlemen;" the Clerk would qualify the witnesses with much seriousness, and all present would take intense interest in the proceedings.

It may appear exceedingly childish to the reader, that men could find pleasure in such matters, but every one who has been in captivity knows how valuable is esteemed every diversion which tends to beguile the tedious hours.

There were several Debating Societies amongst the prisoners, and they contributed to the pleasure and instruction of their members.[6]

[6] Irl R. Hicks, in the introduction and footnotes to his narrative poem, *The Prisoner's Farewell to Johnson's Island, or Valedictory Address to the Young Men's Christian Association of Johnson's Island, Ohio—A Poem,* says that an association known as "The Young Men's Christian Association of Johnson's Island, Ohio" was formed among prisoners of all denominations. The principal aim of the group was to

Decimus et Ultimus Barziza, circa 1880, from a painting in the "Hall of Fame," Jury Assembly Room, Harris County Civil Courts Building, Houston, Texas.

Barziza Family Plot in Glenwood Cemetery, Houston, Texas.

There was, likewise, a Thespian Band, who, under the circumstances, played some very successful pieces. Writing was a favorite occupation with many of the prisoners, and as I have on hand two stray pieces of poetical effusions, I will give them in this place. They are by different authors.

MY LOVE AND I

My Love reposes on a rosewood frame—
 A bunk have I;
A couch of feathery down fills up the same—
 Mine's straw, but dry.
She sinks to sleep at night with scarce a sigh;
With waking eyes I watch the hours creep by.

My Love her daily dinner takes in state—
 And so do I (?).
The richest viands flank her silver plate—
 Coarse grub have I.
Pure wine she sips, with ease her thirst to slake—
I pump my drink from Erie's limpid Lake.

My Love has all the world at will to roam—
 Three acres I:
She goes abroad, or quiet sits at home—
 So can not I.
Bright angels watch around her couch at night—
A Yank, with loaded gun, keeps me in sight.

A thousand weary miles now stretch between
 My Love and I:
To her, this wintry night, cold, calm, serene,
 I waft a sigh;
And hope, with all my earnestness of soul,
To-morrow's mail will bring me my parole.

---

look after the interests of the sick and needy among the prisoners, but the society also cultivated religious, social, and literary interests among its members. Its constitution required an original address or essay to be read at each weekly meeting by a chosen member or invited friend. Many addresses, like that by Hicks, were in verse.

There's hope ahead. We'll meet again—
  My love and I:
We'll wipe away all tears of sorrow then.
  Her love-lit eye
Will all my weary troubles then beguile,
And keep this wayward Reb from Johnson's Isle.

The other is entitled

THE BATTLE OF GETTYSBURG

'Twas when the harvest-sun shone out on rip'ning fields of
  grain;
And when the Summer sky looked down on blooming hill
  and plain;
The soil of Pennsylvania felt the tread of armed men,
Whose shouts were echoed fast and far from hill-top unto
  glen.
Whence come these pouring legions? do they thirst for
  blood or spoil?
Can a conqueror's flatt'ring smile repay them for their toil?
No! they come in full majesty of justice and of right,
'Tis in the cause of Freedom, they have armed them for
  the fight.
And lo! in July's scorching sun the Southern Cross waves
  far
From those dear homes they've left behind the dreadful path
  of war.
And Gettysburg shall witness bear, for long years yet to
  come,
To the might of Southern freemen who battle for their home.
Behold the peaceful, smiling fields, the forests fresh and
  green!
And mark the glitt'ring bayonet—the sword, whose polished
  sheen
Reflects the glancing rays that shall, ere evening close the
  day,
Look down upon the rival hosts in battle's fierce array.

84

The black-mouthed cannon frowning stands upon the rising
  knoll,
Ready to vomit forth its fires; hark! now the lengthened roll
Of the alarming drum calls up the soldier to his feet;
Whilst dashing hither, thither past on chargers strong and
  fleet,
The Aides and couriers fly with frantic speed along the ranks.
The army, like a stream that swells to burst its fett'ring banks,
Seems leaning, pressing close to catch the echoes of the gun
Whose roar shall harshly tell them that the battle has begun.
Now the din of battle swells and is borne upon the breeze,
And the hurtling balls come crashing among the forest trees,
The shrapnel opens with a scream, the smoke makes thick
  the air,
Now, Northern, Southern women, weep! who have a loved
  one there.
But see the red cross of the South! on the heights 'tis waving,
Borne by the brave Confed'rates, who, the dire storm are
  braving
Against the odds that round them pour in swift increasing
  tide,
And the fiends upon the storm of the battle seem to ride.
Now, our men are full upon them with cheers that rend the
  sky;
Press on ye fearless soldiers, for ye do not fear to die;
Yet further, faster on! for the victory's not yet won;
But lo! behind the routed ranks increasing thousands come,
They hurl our worn and tired men back with the force of
  numbers,
Back o'er the bloodly ground which their fallen dead en-
  cumber.
Ah Pickett! you may well regret and weep your gallant slain;
Yet proudly did you bear yourself amid the leaden rain.
Virginia mourns her priceless sons, who, on this bloody field,
A sacrifice unto her name did here their spirits yield.

There were Ewell, Hill and Longstreet, whose paths were
   thickly strewn
With the dead and dying, upon whose features shone
The spirit of the Southron proud, defiant to the last.
The star of our Confederacy was with a shadow cast!
Brave Hood, the dashing warrior, who never knew defeat,
How many hundreds of your braves you never more shall
   greet!
Here, your Georgians, Alabamians, Arkansans, Texans too,
Have, as you always boasted, even to the death proved true.
And Lee, the peerless chieftain, how throbbed his great heart
   then!
But God himself disposes of what is proposed by men.
South Carolina, Mississippi, along with Tennessee,
Have nobly helped our straining ship upon this bloody sea.
And slandered North Carolina, you've this day given the lie
To the baseless fabrications echoed by low and high.
On every field your rifles have added to the slaughter,
Reeking in which your Pettigrew breathed last at Falling
   Water.
Wherever Southern blood's been spilt in most unstinted tide,
The banner of the old North State has always streamed in
   pride.
And ye sons of Louisiana! to give you praise were vain;
Your deeds have made you famous from the mountains to
   the main.
And Florida, she, too, was there, and bore her part that day,
And Maryland left many a son to mingle with the clay.
The three days contest now had closed; the baffled host moved
   back
Towards the swift Potomac wave, yet leaving in their track
The marks of desolating war which warned our vandal foes,
That 'till our independence 's gained, we'll never, never
   close
Our hands in friendship's kindly grasp with those who have
   enkindl'd
These fires of hate; and yet, again, shall woman's wails, com-
   mingl'd

86

With our victorious shouts in far off Northern lands recall
The booming of our guns whose echoes waked their capitol.
Forever float the banner of the brave! and may that God
Who rules above, and with full wisdom wields his chast'ning
    rod,
Support us in our battles fierce and dark extremity,
And grant that in the glorious end our people shall be free.
But if our cruel fate is yet to be at last o'erborne
By overpowering numbers, then, let that strip'd flag be torn
And rent as by the gale! May that whole nation then expire
In the same crackling flames with which they light our fun'ral
    pyre!

Chapter Sixth.

Fort Delaware—Point Lookout.

T HAPPENED to be my good fortune not to go to Fort Delaware during my involuntary stay in the North. But this place is spoken of by all who have been confined there as a perfect hell on earth. The Yankee commander, who now wears the epaulettes of a brigadier-general, Shæff,[1] was formerly a lager-beer vender in St. Louis, and later a waiting servant at Willard's, in Washington. The

[1] Albin Francisco Schoepf, born in Podgorze, Poland, 1822, received military education at an Austrian academy. He worked his way up to major in the Polish Legions during the Hungarian revolution, was exiled to Turkey after suppression of the revolt, and became an artillery instructor in the Ottoman service. He came to America in 1851, without resources or friends, and took a job as a porter in a Washington hotel. His military bearing attracted the attention of Joseph Holt, patent commissioner, who made him a draftsman in the patent office. When Holt became Secretary of War under Buchanan, his protégé was transferred to the War Department. Schoepf was appointed a brigadier general at the opening of the Civil War. After making a reputation with his victory at Wild Cat Camp, Kentucky, he commanded a division at Perryville. Soon after, he resigned his command, partly because of deafness from a wound, partly from disgust at the intrigues revealed at the court-martial of General Don Carlos Buell. In 1863 he became commander of the Federal prison at Fort Delaware, where he seems to have served the remainder of the war (Ella Lonn, *Foreigners in the Union Army and Navy*, pp. 211 and 610).

whole place was a bed of mud and filth; our men actually went bare-footed and their pants rolled up, when walking in the yard. The filth and offal of the prison were mingled with the water they drank, and hundreds died of disease contracted therefrom. The sentinels shoot them down without mercy, and their condition is a burning disgrace to any civilized government. When some of our officers and soldiers were removed to Johnson's Island, the bloated Dutch general required them to take a parole not to attempt to escape, although they were under a strong guard, and swore that he would send those who refused in chains. The prisoners were half fed and almost naked, as they allowed no contributions to come into them. Many have found a watery grave in their attempts to escape, rather than remain and die by piece meal.

Point Lookout, in Maryland, at the mouth of the Potomac, was not much better than Fort Delaware. Point Lookout is the depot for all non-commissioned officers and privates. That is to say, that the majority of them are kept here. The prisoners were crowded in tents, and underwent many privations and sufferings. The treatment they received at the hands of those in authority was absolutely barbarous.

Reward was given for crime. It was understood that any sentinel who shot a prisoner, "consistently with orders," should be awarded by promotion or money; and it may be fairly presumed that the hirelings, thus licensed, often used their power cruelly and wantonly.

They were allowed only one blanket to several men, and their sufferings from cold were intense. The little wood they used was picked up by the prisoners, or doled out to them niggardly.

Beast [Maj. Gen. B. F.] Butler used occasionally to pay them a visit, and as he passed through he was greeted by thousands of indignant and scornful voices. They would cry out, "here comes the man that makes war on women." "Where is that piano you stole in New Orleans?" "Why didn't you come to see us when we had arms in our hands?" [2]

On these occasions the beast would take little time in his tour of inspection, and beat a hasty retreat. The negro sentinels could not quite overcome their raising, and would often say to a prisoner, when he was outside the line, "Massa git in dar, git in dar."

The prisoners had all sorts of diversions. The streets and tents were named. Gambling was a favorite pastime; thousands of dollars were won and lost daily. Money fluctuated in value

[2] Major General Benjamin Franklin Butler, U.S.V., was probably the most thoroughly despised by Confederate soldiers of any Union officer, at this stage of the war. A former member of the Massachusetts Legislature and brigadier of militia, he became a major general on May 16, 1861. According to Hans L. Trefousse (*Ben Butler: The South Called Him Beast!*, pp. 65–145), his military record was unimpressive. He took possession of New Orleans, May 1, 1862, after Admiral Farragut's fleet had virtually captured the city, and at once instituted a very strict military government. He armed the free Negroes and forced rich secessionists to contribute heavily to support of the poor. His dictatorial rule of the city made him thoroughly hated throughout the South and aroused much opposition in the North. He summarily sentenced and hanged a civilian, William Mulford, on suspicion of having led the group who tore down the United States flag from the Mint. He issued an obnoxious order, General Order No. 28, "intended to prevent soldiers from being insulted by women," and seized $800,000 held in custody by the Dutch consul. After a Washington investigation, the money was returned and Butler recalled. Butler's infamous General Order No. 28 (B. F. Butler, *Butler's Book*, p. 418), because of which Jefferson Davis declared him an outlaw and put a price of $10,000 on his head, not only was inflamatory, but contained an amusing malapropism: "As the officers and soldiers of the United States have been subject to repeated insults from the women (calling themselves ladies) of New Orleans, in return for the most scrupulous non-interference and courtesy on our part, it is ordered that hereafter when any female shall, by word, gesture or movement, insult or show contempt for any officer or soldier of the United States, she shall be regarded and held liable to be treated as a woman of the town plying her avocation."

daily. Confederate money was worth from four to seven cents on the dollar, and rose or fell with the prospects of exchange, removal, or with the state of the campaign and the New York markets.

Out of so large a number,[3] as would be expected, a great many took the oath of allegiance,[4] but the per centum was small.

I have seen communications even in the Northern papers, giving accounts of the horrible treatment of the men at Fort Delaware and Point Lookout. The truth is, that the Yankees actually tried to force them to take the oath, by starvation, cold, and ill-treatment. Hundreds accepted the oath for no other purpose than to be released, and stated to their comrades that they would not be bound by it.

So great was the desire to be free from these places, that when a few drew lots to be exchanged, the fortunate ones were offered thousands of dollars for their chance.

I was told by an intelligent and truthful prisoner that he had seen a Yankee corporal beat one of our men over the shoulders with the flat part of a sword, for no other reason than that the prisoner was sick and failed to get in ranks to roll-call in time.

This, though, is but one of the thousand instances of cruelty which could be mentioned.

And notwithstanding all this the Northern papers were continually filled with horrible accounts of the treatment their men

---

[3] There were 40,000 Confederate prisoners in possession of the Federal government and 13,000 Federals in Confederate hands, in October, 1863 (Gen. Clement A. Evans [ed.], *Confederate Military History,* I, 482).

[4] An amnesty proclamation by President Lincoln, December 8, 1863, tendered pardon to individuals who took an oath to support the Constitution, all acts of Congress, and all proclamations having reference to slaves. All Confederates were eligible, except military officers above the rank of colonel in the army or lieutenant in the navy, or any who had resigned from the U.S. services to enter the Confederate service, or any who had treated captured Negro soldiers in any way other than as prisoners of war (*ibid.,* p. 486).

received in Richmond, and urged upon the authorities to use the utmost rigor with ours.

Their columns were taken up with the accounts of Yankee preachers who had been released from Richmond, and who publicly uttered the most improbable falsehoods.

I saw the statement of a Chaplain, who declared that he had seen men on Belle Isle *die of starvation,* and that he has seen them clutch at a piece of crust in their dying agonies.

So much for Yankee humanity and truthfulness!

Chapter Seventh.

Johnson's Island—Arrival of more Prisoners—
Notables in the Prison—Confederates under
Sentence of Death—Gambling—The Choctaw
Indian Captain—Religious Exercises—Prison
Hospital—Grave-Yard—Ill-treatment—Snow-
fight—Campaign between Vallandigham and
Brough.

UT TO RETURN to Johnson's Island, with which most
of this narrative is connected.

Officers were continually arriving from the armies
east and west, among them were the General and
his officers who surrendered themselves at Cumberland Gap,
and thus gave the enemy possession of the most important
position in that part of Tennessee.

There were five brigadier-generals and one major-general
from our armies confined here.

Major-General J. R. [Isaac R.] Trimble [Ewell's Div. of
A. P. Hill's Corps], of Maryland, is a man somewhat advanced
in age, healthy and stoutly built, and has always borne a
high reputation as a soldier. He lost a leg at Gettysburg.

Brigadier-General J. J. Archer [Archer's Tenn. Brigade of
A. P. Hill's Corps], of Maryland, was captured in the first day's
fight at Gettysburg. He is a small, dark complexioned man, and
has an eye full of lurking mischief—keen, piercing and pas-
sionate. He is always calm, easy and affable.

Brigadier-General [William N. R.] Beall [Arkansas Brigade], of Louisiana [Little Rock, Arkansas], was captured at Port Hudson [Louisiana, July 9, 1863]. He is scarcely the medium size—quick, active and intelligent.

Brigadier-General [J. R.] Jones, of Virginia, was formerly the commander of a brigade in Jackson's old division. He is a short, thick-set man, and an agreeable companion.

Brigadier-General J. W. Frazer will be known as the officer who surrendered Cumberland Gap to [Maj. Gen. A. E.] Burnside without a fight. His conduct was severely censured by almost every one. I have heard from good authority that he stated that, previous to his surrender, he invited a free expression of opinion of his officers, and only one, a lieutenant-colonel, said fight. Gen. Frazer is a tall, fine-looking man, dark hair and eyes, and hails from Memphis, Tennessee.

Brigadier-General M. Jeff. Thompson, of Missouri [State Guard], was captured very suddenly and unexpectedly to himself in Arkansas, while he was in the act of planning an expedition against the Yankees. Jeff is long, lean, restless, and the most incessant talker in the "bull-pen." His mouth is very large, his utterance rapid, and his gesticulation vehement. He is fond of jokes and anecdotes, and is always in the best of spirits. He was very popular with his fellow captives, and had a tact of getting along well with the Yankees.

Hundreds of others were there known more or less to fame; among them was Col. J. Lucius Davis [Tenth Virginia Cavalry], of Richmond, Virginia, who, the Yankees think, put the rope around John Brown's neck, and whom they wanted to mob in Pittsburg, when he was being carried to Point Lookout.[1]

[1] This was erroneous. Colonel J. Lucius Davis was commander of the Virginia militia in the Charleston area during the early days of the disturbances following the arrest of John Brown, but was replaced by Major General William B. Taliaferro before the hanging (Allan Keller, *Thunder at Harper's Ferry*, pp. 219–221). The rope was placed around

I have before spoken of the men who were confined apart from the rest, and who were under sentence of death. We were not allowed any communication with them, but could see them, daily, in front of their cells, with their balls upon the shoulders, walking around their little prison-house. One of these men was brought to the hospital block on account of severe illness.

I heard he was there, and having some curiosity to know something more of these poor unfortunates, I went to him, sat by his bed-side, and wrote down the following statement. His name was John Marrs.

Statement of John Marrs.

He is originally from Fayette county, Virginia. He had five brothers in the Confederate service. He was a private in Co. "I," 2d Kentucky infantry, and was captured at the battle of Murfreesboro, January, 1863. He was paroled by his captors, yet still held as a prisoner and under guard.

He made his escape on his way to Camp Douglas in Illinois. Whilst making his way back to our lines, he was recaptured in Kentucky, carried to Cincinnati, tried by a drunken court-martial, who held their sessions over a bar-room, and condemned to be hung under Burnside's death order, No. 38.[2] This was on the

---

John Brown's neck by John W. Campbell, high sheriff, Jefferson County, Virginia (*ibid.*, pp. 267, 271.)

[2] Major General Ambrose E. Burnside's General Order No. 38, dated from Headquarters of the Department of the Ohio, Cincinnati, April 13, 1863, states (*War of the Rebellion: Official Records,* Series 2, V, 480):

Hereafter, all persons found within our lines who commit acts for the benefit of the enemies of our country will be tried as spies or traitors and if convicted will suffer death. This order includes the following class of persons:

Carriers of secret mails.

Writers of letters sent by secret mails.

Secret recruiting officers within our lines.

Persons who have entered into an agreement to pass our lines for the purpose of joining the enemy.

first of May, his trial lasting about two hours. The officers of the command that recaptured him, were the only witnesses against him. He had borne a fictitious name to escape detection by those who might know him in Kentucky, but gave in his true name after the trial, or during it. He was permitted to make a statement before the Court; he stated that he was an enlisted soldier in the Confederate army, when and by whom he was captured, and referred them to where his name could be found as a prisoner of war. Notwithstanding all this, they sentenced him to be hung on the 29th of May. He was brought to Johnson's Island in chains on the 15th of May, the day on which two Confederate officers were executed on the Bay shore by order of Gen. Burnside. Two other men, also under sentence, came with him, viz: George P. Sims, aged 28 years, of Bourbon county, Kentucky, and Wm. S. Burgess, aged 22, of Harrison county, Kentucky.

Here was, also, Thomas M. Campbell, of Nicholas county, Kentucky, awaiting sentence. Sims was a discharged Confederate soldier from 1st Kentucky infantry; Burgess was and is a soldier of Duke's regiment; Campbell was a discharged lieutenant from the 1st Kentucky Rifles.

At this time the little houses inside the prison had not been built, and they were confined in solitary cells, under the room of the officer of the guard. Each was heavily ironed and thrust into

Persons found concealed within our lines belonging to the service of the enemy, and in fact all persons found improperly within our lines who could give private information to the enemy.

All persons within our lines who harbor, protect, conceal, feed, clothe or in any way aid the enemies of our country.

The habit of declaring sympathies for the enemy will not be allowed in this department. Persons committing such offenses will be at once arrested, with a view to being tried as above stated, or sent beyond our lines into the lines of their friends.

It must be distinctly understood that treason expressed or implied will not be tolerated in this department.

All officers and soldiers are strictly charged with the execution of this order.

a cell about four feet high and five feet long, with a slight crack for light. They remained here until the cells were built inside the prison-yard. The day before their day of execution, they received notice that the President had postponed it until the 5th of June. It was again postponed, and this time until further orders, as it now stands. The house in which they have been confined since May, 1863, is divided into eight small compartments or cells, each about seven feet high, two and a half feet wide, and long enough to lie down in; a little window, about six inches in length, and one inch and a half in width, admits light and air. At sunset each is locked up separately in his little cell.

Each had a ball, weighing sixty-four pounds, with a chain attached, six feet long, on one leg; shackles riveted upon their ankles, with about fourteen inches play, and handcuffs on the wrists. During the day, they were allowed to sling their balls on their shoulders, and walk within the stakes, a space of about fifteen feet square. They had no straw to lie upon, nor did they have any fire until November. They suffered very much with cold last Fall; their cells were very damp, the floor being on the ground. Sometimes the other prisoners could be seen walking in the lot without coats, whilst they would be shivering with cold.

At times they are lively and jolly; again, they are moody, silent and well nigh crazed. They read, sleep, talk and think, and have learned to look upon death with perfect indifference —nay, as a solace and a comfort. In reply to a question, whether they were professors of religion, Marrs replied, that they were not members of the church, but were not afraid to die; but that this feeling of indifference to death is much the result of despair and recklessness. They care very little whether their sentence shall be carried out or not.

Thus runs one truthful account of the despotism of the Federal Government; but one hundredth part cannot be told, and much will never be known. Hundreds of victims are languishing in prison whose fate will never come to light.

I will say, that upon my arrival in the Confederacy, I laid before the Secretary of War the above statement, in order, if possible, that some proper steps might be taken in behalf of our suffering people.

During the Fall, our little world, the prison, was full of fun, business and gambling. The latter was a common pastime. It was very common to see a colonel sitting at a table dealing "faro;" whilst officers of all grades bet at it, or played "poker."

The gamblers controlled the capital; some lucky ones had won twenty or thirty thousand dollars each. This practice was carried to an extent hardly credible. I have seen "poker playing" in the same room where preaching was being carried on. And this reminds me of a poor Choctaw Indian Captain from the western army, who died here. Amongst his papers was found an article styled "Savage and Civilized." After stating his journey to Johnson's Island, and the curiosity of the whites to see him, he said he found himself at last amongst hundreds of high officers, representing the "civilized" white people; and that he attended church in the prison: while the minister was speaking the audience were engaged in all sorts of disorder, laughing and talking, and adds that when he attends church in his country, he hears no one talk except the minister; that Choctaws keep silent, "and yet," he concluded, "they call me Indian —savage." What a just and scathing satire from a poor Indian!

We had the privilege of religious exercises almost daily. All denominations were represented, and indulged in their own peculiar services. We very often had revivals of religion, and very many were converted.

We had, too, a good hospital. One whole block was reserved for this purpose. It was under the charge of our army surgeons, until they were specially exchanged, when it was taken charge of by officers who were physicians by profession. The whole was under the general supervision of a Yankee surgeon, who visited it two or three times a week. The supply of medicines was very scanty. We furnished nurses, cooks, &c., by hiring our own officers. The most common disease amongst us was erysipelas, though we had small-pox all the time. The latter cases were taken out of the yard to an out-house. We had a grave-yard for the burial of our dead, about three hundred yards distant; we bought plank and had it fenced in, and laid out conveniently and tastefully, and marked all the graves.

Many a rebel lies peacefully sleeping there on the bleak shore of Lake Erie.[3]

We were often annoyed by the insolence of the Yankees; and I will give a few instances which will exhibit their meanness.

A brigadier-general happened to be a little late at roll-call, whereupon the corporal very insolently informed him that he had to do some work with pick and spade as a punishment; the general refused to do it, and was sent out and confined in a cell in consequence.

Brigadier-General Archer bribed a sentinel to permit him to escape. At the time appointed, the sentinel appeared, assisted him over the fence, received the bribe—a gold watch and some

---

[3] Colonel Charles W. Hill, 128th Ohio Volunteer Infantry, commanding Johnson's Island, reported to Brigadier General H. W. Wessells, Washington, D.C., Inspector and Commanding General of Prisoners, December 17, 1864, that "up to the present date 7,377 prisoners of war have been received at this depot, among whom 198 deaths have occurred . . ." (*Official Records*, Series 2, VII, 1235).

Morton Brown, 106 East 18th Street, Austin, states that his father, the late First Lieutenant William Morton Brown, Rockbridge Artillery, Army of Northern Virginia, C.S.A., who was also a prisoner at Johnson's Island, told him that when the ground froze solidly during the winter and graves could not be dug, the bodies of dead prisoners were stacked in the hallways between prison blocks. The prisoners had to pass between the stacks of bodies on their way to meals. At first, he said, many appetites were curbed, but in time the living became accustomed to the sight of their dead, stacked like cordwood in the hallways.

three hundred dollars—and delivered him over to the officer of the guard, who put him in a cell. The officer had colluded with the sentinel, and between them they made a good speculation at the expense of honor, and, no doubt, enjoyed the money.

A certain colonel made his escape, and succeeded in reaching Newark, in Ohio, where he was arrested, and sent back to prison. A few days after, he received a note from Col. Pierson, the commandant, informing him that the government had incurred an expense of *ten dollars* in his recapture, and that amount would be deducted from the money the colonel had in Pierson's hands.

Col. Pierson did not recognize rank in our officers, but addressed all as Mr.

Our sutler and Pierson had caused to be struck off a photographic picture of the island and prison, thinking that most of the prisoners would like to have some such memento. The price was five dollars, but finding it did not sell, and having received orders to make out rolls of the prisoners, they were afraid they would lose on their pictures, and consequently they would not receive an order on Colonel Pierson, unless the order included three dollars for a picture. We bought from the sutler by giving him an order on Colonel Pierson for the amount of our purchase, as all our money was held by the commandant. But now the sutler was instructed not to sell a prisoner anything unless he also bought a picture at three dollars. So a man could not buy a plug of tobacco unless he also contributed three dollars for the benefit of the sutler and his master.

Truly, this was a Yankee trick!

Many other such meannesses were continually being practiced upon the Confederates.

As winter advanced, prison life became unutterably irksome. The days were spent in restlessness and the nights in wakefulness. In the room in which I was, there was a coal-oil lamp which we had purchased, which gave a beautiful soft light to every portion of the room. I have often lain in my bunk and regarded the different occupations of the inmates of the crowded room. Some were reading, others playing cards or chess, others laughing and talking, others pacing the floor, others singing; and, in short, every employment was indulged in which would tend to beguile the weary, weary hours.

Thoughts of home and friends filled the breasts of all, and many had even given up in despair.

I noticed that the slightest sickness often had the most depressing effect. In fact, the mind was so completely harassed, that even superstition held sway in some instances. I remember the case of a captain. A little bird happened to perch upon his hat one day; he was told by some one, in a careless manner, that this was "a sign of his death." The captain immediately became very melancholy, and in a few days sickened and died.

During the winter we had a great snow-ball battle. The prisoners were divided into two parties, organized into companies and battalions, and for three or four hours they were engaged in a severe and exciting fight.

The Yankees looked on with much merriment, but I can scarcely think they felt entirely at ease, when they heard the yells of the rebels.

Mrs. Pierson used to say she disliked so much to hear the yelling of the rebels; it always made the colonel so uneasy, lest they were preparing for an uprising and outbreak.

The campaign [for governor of Ohio] between [John] Brough and [Clement L.] Vallandigham about this time was one of great bitterness. The abolitionists boldly charged the copperheads with treason and sympathy with the rebels, and the copperheads, in turn, denounced the Administration as imbecile and tyrannous.

After the election, in which Vallandigham was defeated, it was asserted by the democratic press, that the vote for their candidate was much larger than it had been in a preceding election in the Spring, in which they were then successful, and that fraud and stuffing the ballot-box could, alone, have secured the success of Brough.

In truth, popular elections at that time were farces; and the history of them showed the inevitable results of military power. Each party strove to prove its candidate to be a better friend to the soldiers than his opponent. They feared not only the votes, but the bayonets of their own hirelings. The military was flattered, worshipped and dreaded; the people bore the utmost deference, forced, it may have been, to a blue uniform. Nothing could flourish unless it was subsidiary to the military. And the President, who controlled that mighty machinery, was, of course, all-powerful. General orders of a military commander had as much force amongst them as if they had the sanction of Sinai's thunder.

However much moral condemnation we might have for Abraham Lincoln, yet one could but admire the masterly process by which he had changed a free republic to an obsequious despotism. Step by step did this man tread the road to absolute power, and at that time he was enthroned with a sway equal to that of any autocrat of the old world, and had bridled a people, who, three years previous, were the most arrogant, self-willed, and independent nation in existence.

How jealously these people had heretofore watched encroachments of power! And how quick they were to resent supposed national wrongs! Yet Lincoln loomed up the monarch and tyrant, who, instead of being influenced by public opinion, actually moulded it, made men think like he did and act as he required them.

Such wonderful strides towards absolutism by one man against the prejudices and education of twenty millions, must call forth admiration for the subtle policy and diplomacy which accomplished so much.

What will be the sequel? *"Nous verrons."* The hand of fate is on the curtain, and it will soon be torn aside.

Early in the Spring there were a great many rumors afloat—

"grape-vines" we called them. Among them was one to the effect that Beast Butler had been given the control of all prisoners, and that we would be removed to Point Lookout, there to undergo such treatment, as *was alleged,* the Yankees received in Richmond, which was barbarous.

Accordingly, about the ninth of February, about four hundred and fifty officers were chosen, alphabetically, as the first installment, and prepared to move. I was amongst the number.

I give below the official report of Lieut. Col. Pierson, in regard to the number of prisoners. The whole number now at Johnson's Island is claimed as officers; but, in explanation, I will say there are several hundred citizens, militia officers, and ex-officers.

EXTRACT from the Official Report of Lieut. Col. W. S. Pierson, made January 18th, 1864, on being relieved of the command of Johnson's Island, by Brig. Gen. Terry, Commanding Third Division, 6th Corps, U.S. Army. The prison was established in January, 1862.

The whole number of prisoners has been............ 6416
Of which there have been exchanged.............. 2983
Discharged on oath of allegiance, parole and otherwise.. 302
Transferred to other prisons..................... 363
Deaths 149
Shot dead by sentinel........................... 1
Executed 3
Escaped 3
Present, at this time, January 18th, 1862............. 2612–6416

Chapter Eighth.

Departure from Johnson's Island—Plans for
Escape—Escape—Travel through the North and
incidents therein—Arrival in Canada—Montreal—Sleigh Riding—Skating Rinks—British
Soldiers and Citizens—Queen Victoria.

ALL THINGS READY, on the 9th or 10th of February
we took a lasting farewell of Johnson's Island. We
embarked upon a little steamer, and were landed in
Sandusky city.

Great crowds of men, women and children, thronged the
streets. We were in all styles of dress, and carried all sorts of
baggage. We had never seen a child in prison nor a woman; and
it really appeared as if children now walked at an earlier age
than they used to. It looked unnatural to us to see little tiny
things walking and running about. All the women looked pretty
in our eyes—even the naughty ones, who cried out, "look at the
thieves and murderers."

That night we were put in the third story of a large building,
and a jolly night it was; any change was pleasant to us then,
and we really enjoyed it.

I could but be amused at a lieutenant, when some one remarked the condition we would be in, in case of fire; the lieutenant very seriously said: "Well, if the whole earth were to
burn up to-night, I wouldn't be any the loser, provided I saved

this bag," and he touched a huge sack filled with old clothes, books, trumpery, &c.

The next morning found us on the train *en route* for Pittsburg. A lieutenant and myself had made our plans to escape. Accordingly, we got in the same car, and near each other. The plan was, about one o'clock in the night we were to jump out the window. I on one side and he on the other, while our comrades between ourselves and the sentinels stood up, and, pretending to spread their blankets, should thus conceal us.

At the signal, we started; I was detected and ordered back, whilst Lieut. A. succeeded in getting out. He had not a cent of money, but after two months of adventure he arrived safely in the Confederacy.

We arrived at Pittsburg the next evening, and pursued our journey, by night, towards Harrisburg. About three o'clock in the morning, I succeeded in leaping from the window of a box-car, reached the ground, and was soon left by the train. Fortunately, I fell upon a level place, and did not seriously hurt myself. I cannot describe my feelings at this time. I started in a run from the direction of the railroad, and after traveling as well as I could until daybreak, I lay down in the woods and resolved in my mind what was best to be done.

I would have given treasures for a companion at this time, for some one to have advised and counseled with. I had no idea where I was; had five dollars in greenbacks, and was dressed in a suit of citizens' clothes.

I finally resolved to make my way to the railroad, and trust to fate and fortune. I had not gone far before I saw a town ahead, and thinking and hoping it was Harrisburg, I remembered I had money enough to take me to Philadelphia. Approaching the town, I asked a lad the time of day as an excuse to stop awhile. I then asked him how far they called it to Philadelphia. "Oh, sir," he replied, "I don't know, but it must be a long way, as it is a hundred miles to Harrisburg." At this piece of information, I was exceedingly disturbed, and longed for a little more money. However, I kept on in the town, quite undetermined as to my action. I was cold and hungry, and passing up the streets of the town, which proved to be Huntingdon,[1] I espied the sign of a lager beer saloon, and went in, took a drink and a cigar, and very unceremoniously sat down before the stove, and assumed an air of familiarity with a bar-room, which was not difficult to do. The proprietor, who was a dutchman, was alone, and soon entered in conversation with me. He told me he was a discharged soldier from some Pennsylvania regiment, and named the campaigns he had passed through. I represented myself as a disabled and discharged soldier from the 2d Massachusetts infantry. We discussed the war prospects, denounced Jeff. Davis and his Cabinet, consigned all the rebels to the devil, and took a drink at the host's expense. I made this place my headquarters; learned from the dutchman the fare to Philadelphia, and the hour at which the train came through. I still did not know what town I was in, and, of course, asked nobody. I heard, however, the dutchman mention the "Globe" as the paper published in the town, and some hours after, I found a paper lying on the counter of a store, and read "The Huntingdon Globe." I was then in Huntingdon, but I had never heard of the place before.

I went out in the street, sought a barber-shop, had my hair cut, and got shaved, and proceeded to a jeweler's to sell a large, plain gold ring.[2]

Judging it would look suspicious for a stranger to offer for sale a ring in a small town like this, I had recourse to strategy.

I walked in the shop, stood over the show-glass, and requested the keeper to show me some gutta-percha rings, that I wished

[1] Huntingdon, Huntingdon County, Pennsylvania, approximately one hundred miles northwest of Harrisburg.

[2] Barziza's father, Phillip Ignatius, had given each of his ten children an identical simple gold ring. A descendant, P. D. Barziza, 3906 Brook-Woods, Houston, has one of these rings today (P. D. Barziza to R. H. S., September 20, 1962).

to purchase one. He accordingly did so, and I pulled off my ring and let it drop on the glass, and put on the other on the same finger. The jeweler took up my ring, and remarked: "This is a very fine ring." "Yes," said I, "what is it worth?" After examining it, he rejoined, "about four and a half in greenbacks." "What is this worth?" said I, meaning the one I then had on. "Fifty cents," said he. "Well," I remarked, "give me the difference, I had as soon wear a gutta percha as a gold ring." He accordingly handed over the money, and I left, went to a restaurant, and indulged in a plate of oysters, took a drink, puffed a cigar, and felt quite happy.

An incident happened, in this connection, which I will not pass over. I was in a barber-shop indulging in a comfortable shave; there were some dozen Yankee officers and soldiers present; the conversation was about the war, and the immense bounties that were offered. I joined in and pretended Yankee, and was particularly severe upon the rebellion. I was interrupted by one of the Yankees, who inquired of me: "Where are you from? Are you not a New Englander?" "Yes," I replied, "I am from Massachusetts. But why do you ask; do you judge so from my dialect?" "Yes," said he, "I know you from your speech." I thought to myself that he was an acute observer—God knows I haven't got much of the Yankee about me, although, on that occasion, I may have tried to appear so, and I had not the slightest objection to be mistaken for one at that particular time. However, I felt much gratified at the prospects of having been temporarily Yankeeized. Late in the evening I went to a hotel and took supper. Whilst sitting in the bar-room after supper, enjoying a cigar, I saw an old man come in, and heard him ask the proprietor to give him supper and lodging; that he was a poor man and had two sons in the army, and was on his way to Pittsburg, where his sons had enlisted, to gain some tidings of them. The proprietor suspected something wrong about the man, and questioned him very closely, and turning to me said: "All he has to do is to write to the regiment, isn't it?" "Certainly," said I, "our postal arrangements are such as that a letter is required only to be addressed to any particular regiment, and it will go safely, whether the command belongs to the eastern or western army." After the old man left, the proprietor remarked to me, "I don't like that man's story." "Nor I," replied I, "there are a great many suspicious characters traveling through the country;" and I settled back in my arm-chair very complacently.

I took the train for Philadelphia at eleven o'clock at night, seated myself beside a Yankee lieutenant, and very soon we made a traveling acquaintance. I had a flask of whiskey of which he partook very sociably. He was on some general's staff at Pittsburg or Harrisburg; and I represented myself as a discharged Massachusetts soldier, and at present connected with a firm in Boston, for which I had been purchasing bacon in Ohio. We talked, and dozed, and drank, until we arrived in Philadelphia.

Here, then, I was in the Quaker city! I had thirty cents, twenty-five of which I spent for a very simple breakfast, and bought a cigar with the remaining five cents, which left me absolutely penniless in a city I had never before been in, save once when I was marched through as a prisoner of war. However, before three hours had passed, I was on the train for New York with fifty dollars in my pocket, and a carpet-bag of clothing. How I made this "raise," it does [not] matter, whether I stole, robbed, begged, or gambled; I know I had it, and made good use of it.

Stopping only a few hours in New York city, I arrived in Troy on Sunday morning, registered an assumed name, hailing from Philadelphia, and remained until Monday morning.

I attended church in Troy, and bowed right reverently as the minister offered up prayer in behalf of Lincoln, and deprecated the terrible sin of the rebellion.

The next morning found me easily sitting in a comfortable car, making all possible speed northward. I usually took a seat near some soldier traveling on furlough, and very soon entered into familiar conversation.

I was, at this time, very uneasy, fearing lest a passport should be required of me when I attempted to cross the line into Canada. Good fortune, however, even provided in this case. At some depot, beyond Burlington, a negro boy got upon the train, and very unceremoniously seated himself by me. I must confess that, at first, I didn't relish the familiarity, but kept my feelings to myself. He soon told me that he was on his way to Montreal, and showed me British papers, certifying that he was one of Her Majesty's subjects, and resident of Montreal, but did not state his color. He seemed to be a half-witted fellow, and told me he only had money sufficient to carry him to Rousse's Point, the boundary between United States and Canada.

Determined to get possession of his papers should I need them, I informed him that I was on my way to Montreal, and that if he stayed with me and looked after my baggage, I would pay his fare. He agreed very readily. But it happened I did not require any papers—only had my baggage examined—and thus had no further use for the sable Canadian. I cannot describe the joy and exuberance of feeling when I was free! On a Canada train, in a foreign country, and under the protection of Her Majesty, the Queen! I could scarcely contain myself; it seemed that I had been born again, and I realized then, for the first time, the inestimable privilege of liberty.

Here, then, I could speak what I chose, go whither I pleased, and was no longer under the insolent *surveillance* of Yankee soldiers. I reached Montreal about ten o'clock at night, during a terrible snow-storm, and being very thinly clad, I suffered intensely. The wind was blowing fearfully, and the air was filled with the dry snow-flakes.

I leaped into a sleigh and bade the driver take me to a hotel. I reached the Doneganna hotel half frozen, got thawed by a huge drink of good brandy, and spent a comfortable night.

When I rose in the morning I began to think of my situation.

I was free, it is true, but I was in a foreign land, among strangers, and had about seven or eight dollars.

Fortune, however, which never deserted me, now showered her favors upon me. I found at the hotel an old college mate, who was in business in the city, and I spent three weeks in Montreal very agreeably.

There was not a wheel to be seen at this time. Traveling was done altogether in sleighs, and were gotten up in the most elegant styles; they were beautifully decorated with costly furs and robes, and drawn by excellent horses.

The principal places of amusement, at this time, were the skating rinks. Rink is a Scotch word, meaning an ice-pond or park. The rink was a large plane of ice, covered over by an extensive building, which was illuminated with gas, and well fitted up for the comfort and convenience of visitors.

Hundreds of skaters, of all ages and sexes, glided like spectres along the smooth surface. I have seen polkas, cotillons, and other dances performed by the skaters, which, to me, appeared wonderful.

Little girls, not more than ten years old, fantastically dressed, skimmed along like fairies, and scarcely seemed to touch the ice. I think it was the most graceful, healthy and innocent exercise I ever saw for females.

A band of music added to the hilarity of the scene, and the night (up to ten o'clock) was spent in joyousness and gaiety. The utmost decorum and order prevailed, and withal, I think a rink filled with a hundred skaters, lighted by the soft beams from gas, enlivened by strains of music, presents one of the most beautiful and attractive scenes I ever beheld.

There were some six or eight thousand troops at Montreal; they had been sent over at the time of the Trent affair.[3] The

[3] On November 8, 1861, the captain of the U.S.S. *San Jacinto* stopped the British mail packet *Trent* en route to England and took from her by force two Confederate agents, Mason and Slidell. Over in London, in the wild haste of what looked to be certain war, they put together

Canadians were very proud of these red-coats; they imagined that they could destroy any quantity of Yankees. In fact, I think the British are the greatest braggarts I ever met with, not even excepting the Yankees. They expressed great admiration for, and, indeed, almost universally sympathized with the South; thought that Southern soldiers fought with great gallantry, but that the huge, strapping six-feet fellows of the Victoria Guard could walk over the Yankees with ease. They regard us as inexperienced in war, but *their* generals and army could very soon make a clean sweep of America.

The truth is, these British are afraid of Yankee Doodle, and their sympathy for us is not so much the result of love for us as hatred for the Yankees. They desire that colossal power on their borders to be broken before it shall swallow up their own fair provinces.

They despise the Yankees; they call them national swindlers. A very intelligent gentleman remarked to me: "Why, sir, these Yankees are a most pestiferous people, shrewd, cunning and energetic. In fixing the boundary between Maine and New Brunswick, they swindled us out of thousands of square miles. Then, again, in the Reciprocity Treaty, by which goods and merchandize, intended for the Canadas, were allowed to be landed in the United States, and shipped here without duty; in return for which, we granted them the right of fishing along a portion of our coast; and, sir, to this day, where one English fishing boat is engaged in that business, there are ten Yankee ones. They are, sir, a grasping, selfish, greedy set. I wish your people would kill them out."

In such style as this does John Bull berate his cousin Jonathan.

The British are devoted to their Queen, and love the English constitution. You may abuse and criticise all the ministers and

an expeditionary force of nearly 15,000 men for British North America. That winter the reinforcements were carried to Canada. Then the United States restored the arrested Southern diplomats and the crisis ended (Donald G. Creighton, *A History of Canada*, p. 287).

departments of the governments, but you must never touch the royal family. The portrait of Her Majesty adorns every public place, from the Parliament down to the lager beer saloons. They speak of her with great reverence. And, indeed, it cannot be doubted that she is a model woman, mother and queen.

In speaking of the morality and purity of her court, a gentleman related me the following incident which occurred soon after her marriage. She had a standing rule in her household that her house should be closed at a certain hour of the night. Prince Albert came home one night after this hour, and found the doors closed and entrance denied him. It created some disturbance, and threatened to bring about a separation, but Her Majesty firmly insisted that this rule of her household should not be relaxed or altered.

I was received very kindly by many of the citizens of Montreal. Among them I shall ever remember Mr. Parsons, the gentlemanly and talented editor of the Evening Telegram. He made me a present of a fine revolver, and has done much for the Confederates and their cause. Other gentlemen, mostly former citizens of the South, rendered great assistance to myself and two other escaped Confederates, and raised money for our journey southward.

Three of us left Montreal together, by way of the Grand Trunk Railway, and, after traveling all night, arrived in Quebec. This city, famed in history for its bloody defence and capture, has the appearance of a very old French town. The streets are very narrow, the houses old-fashioned, and the inhabitants nearly all French.

I visited the defences and the citadel, and stood by the monument of [Gen. James] Wolfe, who fell here.[4]

The city is placed upon a high bluff, commanding the river

[4] Gen. James Wolfe, British commander, was killed September 13, 1759, before Quebec, in the battle of the Plains of Abraham. General Montcalm, the French commander, was killed in the same battle (William L. Langer [ed.], An Encyclopedia of World History, p. 516).

St. Lawrence for miles, and would be a formidable place to reduce.

Arriving at Riviere Du Loup, we took sleighs, and continued this mode of travel nearly all the way to Halifax, a distance of about five hundred miles. This was a novel way of traveling, but a very comfortable one, we being provided with good warm robes and furs. In this manner I traveled Canada East, New Brunswick and Nova Scotia.

Chapter Ninth.

St. John, N.B.—The Chesapeake Case—Halifax, N.S.—St. Georges, Bermuda—Blockade Running—Chase by Blockader—Arrival in Dixie.

ARRIVING at St. John, New Brunswick, I found the people in a state of high excitement, in relation to the case of the captors of the Chesapeake.

It will be remembered that a few Confederates took passage on this steamship from Boston or New York, to Portland, Maine, and whilst at sea they captured the vessel. The ship was afterwards retaken by a Federal man-of-war in the waters near St. John. Most of the Confederates escaped; but several (three I believe) were arrested by the police magistrate in St. John, and ordered to be delivered over to the United States. Before they were handed over, however, they were taken before Judge [W. J.] Ritchie [of the Supreme Court of New Brunswick], on *habeas corpus,* and set at liberty. The inhabitants exhibited much sympathy for them, and declared they should not, in any event, be given up to the United States.

The men being released, betook themselves off, and I suppose reached the Confederacy in safety. The capture of this ship was a daring achievement; but, by bad management, the fruits of it were lost.

Halifax is a pleasant city, affording an excellent harbor, and has a great deal of trade. At this place I met Hon. J. P. Holcombe,[1] and Beverly Tucker, Esq., of Virginia.[2] The former came on to put in a claim on behalf of the government of the Confederate States, for the steamship Chesapeake, which was captured by Confederates. The ship, however, had left a few days before under convoy of the U.S. gun-boat, Miami. So bitter is the feeling in this place against the Yankees, that a Federal officer cannot walk the streets, with uniform on, without being subject to insult even from the little boys in the city. I remember when the Miami anchored off the city; the wharf-

[1] On December 7, 1863, the coastal steamer, *Chesapeake,* which plied the route between New York and Portland, was seized by a group of young men, mostly Confederate sympathizers from Nova Scotia, under the leadership of John C. Braine, a twenty-three–year–old professional artist who claimed to have been born in London, but who had spent much of his time in the South. The steamer was recaptured by Northern warships in a Nova Scotian harbor and those conspirators who had not escaped were put in irons in the hold of the *Dacotah.* Nova Scotians freed the prisoners and held the *Chesapeake,* insisting that any trial of the matter must take place in Halifax. The incident created tension between the North and England, which the Confederacy sought to heighten. Early in 1864, James P. Holcombe, law professor from the University of Virginia and member of the House of Representatives of the Confederate Congress, was sent to Halifax, to determine how the Chesapeake affair might best be turned to Southern advantage and to organize some means of transport to the South for stranded Confederate soldiers who had escaped Federal prisons into Canada (Robin W. Winks, *Canada and the United States: The Civil War Years,* pp. 244–266).

[2] Nathaniel Beverly Tucker, who had been professor of law at William and Mary when Barziza was a student there, was undoubtedly known to him. Tucker had been one of Williamsburg's best-known citizens, one of the leading Southern writers on political subjects in the period before the Civil War, and a close advisor of another Williamsburg neighbor, President John Tyler. Tucker had served as a consul to Liverpool under President Buchanan, and now was in Halifax, at the request of Jefferson Davis, negotiating a contract for the Confederacy to exchange Southern cotton for Union bacon through the Canadas on a pound-for-pound basis (*ibid.,* p. 297).

rats and other boys collected together at night, and with torches, drums, clubs, &c., went to the wharf and invited the crew to come ashore for a fight, which the Yankees prudently declined. The defences of Halifax are admirable and formidable. Here, as everywhere, the most thorough contempt was expressed for the Yankees, and especially on the part of the officers of the British army, who think that the present war is not much of an affair; that the men on either side fail to come up with the bayonet, and decide matters as they would do, and as they did at Inkerman, Malakoff, and the Redan.[3] I almost wished that the Yankees would fight and whip them, so as to undeceive them.

I met and conversed with a great many Yankees who were in Halifax. They were usually polite and well-behaved, but when they were disposed to be otherwise, we, three or four being together, would very soon compel them to be so. Several, however, of the more forward Yankees were taken to task while we [were] here, and even they afterwards were very discreet both in their language and conduct. I must not fail, in this connection, to make mention of a gentleman who resides in Halifax, and who has rendered invaluable aid to our people. I refer to Alex. Keith, jr.[4] His services merit a handsome reward from our government, which, it is to be hoped, he will some day get.

[3] Battle of Inkerman Plateau, November 5, 1854; Battle of Towers Malakoff, September 8, 1855; Battle of Redan, September 8, 1855; all in Crimean War.

[4] Alexander Keith, Jr., of Halifax was more than a sympathetic neutral. At a trial in Halifax, in January, 1864, over the *Chesapeake* affair, it developed that Keith had acted as a relay agent for messages between the Confederate agents in Canada and Richmond (Winks, *Canada and the United States,* p. 258).

James P. Holcombe, chief of the Confederate mission to Canada, listed Keith as one of several prominent men of Halifax who "have given money, time and influence without reserve, as if our cause had been that of their own country" (Holcombe to Confederate Secretary of State Judah P. Benjamin, in report on the *Chesapeake* affair, April 1,

There were several blockade runners in this port undergoing repairs, among them was the famous City of Petersburg.

After three weeks delay in Halifax, I shipped aboard the royal mail steamship Alpha, in company with some half dozen Confederates, and after a passage of about four days arrived at St. Georges, in the Bermuda Islands. Here, everything looked like Summer, though it was the month of February. The Bermudas are a cluster of many small islands of delightful climate and fertile soil.

The British have a garrison at St. Georges. I saw the Confederate flag flying from six or seven steamers in this port, and saw the stars and stripes, "alone in its glory," floating from an insignificant looking brig.

Our agent at this place had under his charge a large amount of stores and munitions of war belonging to the Confederacy.

St. Georges is a delightful spot, but the inhabitants are not much refined. A great many negroes swagger about the streets in the insolence of freedom; and a majority of them are depraved, prostituted and filthy. I here saw the renowned Capt. [John Newland] Maffit [, Jr.], of the Florida. He is a small man, beyond middle age, quiet and easy in demeanor, and is said to be very fond of "his tea."

It was one evening, early in April, I stood upon the deck of the steamship Edith,⁵ Capt. Gregory, and bidding farewell to St. Georges, she put to sea, and headed for the coast of North Carolina. About twelve o'clock that night I was roused from a reverie whilst smoking on deck, by the voice of the captain, calling all hands on deck, and I was told the ship was sinking. As I had never been shipwrecked, and had heard and read of its dangers, I was very considerably disturbed; but managed to get down in the cabin, and got my carpet-bag, which contained

---

1864; cited in *Official Records of the Union and Confederate Navies in the War of the Rebellion*, Series 1, II, 553).

⁵ Blockade runner, later converted into Confederate cruiser, *Chicamauga*.

some papers, and made myself ready to leap into the life-boat whenever the ship should be found to be settling. As I stood upon the deck, I fancied that I could see her gradually getting lower and lower in the water. It was soon discovered, however, that the cause of alarm was a quantity of water that had dashed in through the hawser ports, which had been negligently left open. Truly, it was a great relief to us all. I had resigned myself to another adventure, but, thank God, was spared it. Blockade runners keep a man at the mast-head during the day, who reports every vessel in sight. If a steamer is discovered, without waiting to find what she is, the ship is hauled off, and runs her out of sight. So it sometimes happens that two blockade runners are running from each other. All of these ships are built very light, carry powerful machinery, and are very fast. They are painted white from stem to stern, so as not to be so easily discovered at sea. The Yankee blockaders give chase to everything they see.

On the second morning out from St. Georges, we espied at daylight three steamers, all of which bore down upon us. We immediately prepared for a chase and fired up. In a few hours we had run out of sight of two of them, but the third, a large paddle-wheel, still kept up in our wake. And for thirteen hours did this chase continue, when night coming on we changed our course and slipped the Yankee. Our ship was a double-screw, and made fifteen miles an hour throughout the whole day. Thanks to the good ship, and the perseverance and seamanship of the officers of the Edith, we escaped this fellow. We purposed making the coast that night, but a terrific thunder storm drove us to sea again. What a wild, fearful and sublime scene is a thunder storm at sea in the darkness of the night! The flashes of the lightning illuminated for some moments the whole heavens, exposing to the view the black and seething waters, rolling in billows mountain high and dashing the spray far up into the air.

What an insignificant thing is man when cast upon the "waste of waters." His ship a mere speck, as the heaving billow toys with its weakness; now lurched high and trembling upon the crest of a wave, now settling, plunging down deep in the watery valley.

I never see the ocean in its terrible grandeur, its wild and playful moods, its ever continuous heaving, without being impressed with an awe of that great being who holds the waters in the "hollow of his hand," and recalling the sublime apostrophe of Byron—"Roll on, thou deep and dark blue ocean, roll," &c.

We crept under the guns of Fort Fisher [6] about one o'clock at night, and were safe.

When we rose next morning, we could see the blockaders in the offing, and as they moved towards us the guns of the fort thundered their warnings. After an absence of nearly a year in the enemy's land, I found myself again in the ever loved land of the South. My heart bounded with joy to see the gray jackets again, and to hear the words of defiance spoken against our foes. And now I stepped upon the soil of freemen, and thanked God I was one of them. I was now repaid for all toil and adventure, and forgetting the scenes of pleasure and prosperity I had lately seen elsewhere, felt proud of the soiled coats and unbleached shoes of my own brothers in Dixie.

In closing this narrative, hastily written and crude as it is, I would fain exhort the gallant men in the South to be firm, hopeful and confident. Your fame is praised and sang in other tongues and in other climes; your deeds have made you nobly historic, and the world looks on in wonder and admiration at

[6] Constructed in 1861 at Confederate Point (now Federal Point), North Carolina, near the north entrance to the Cape Fear River, Fort Fisher was the largest earthwork fort in the Confederacy. Until the last few months of the Civil War it kept Wilmington open to the blockade runners from Bermuda, on which the Confederacy relied heavily to supply its armies. It was also the terminus for the return route established for escaped prisoners, from Canada, via Nova Scotia and Bermuda (*Fort Fisher, State Historic Site,* issued by State Department of Archives and History, North Carolina).

your sufferings, privations and sacrifices. The goal is almost won. The names of Lee, Jackson and Beauregard, are as familiar in the old world as those of Napoleon and Wellington. Southern heroism is honored throughout the earth, and her faithful sons are welcomed in every land.

May the cloud soon be dispersed, and the genial rays of peace beam in splendor upon this our down-trodden but worthy land. May war speedily be satiated with blood, and peace, ease and plenty, descend upon our noble soldiery and people.

Chapter Tenth.

Return to Virginia—Appearance of Richmond —Preparations of Grant—The Battle of the Wilderness—The Battle of Spottsylvania Court-House—Battle of Coal Harbor—Grant's character—Gen. Lee and the Army of Northern Virginia.

NCE MORE I found myself upon the soil of the "Old Dominion"—"sacred" indeed now, as men of every civilized nation on earth repose in death beneath it. Historic Virginia, ever proud and defiant to foes, foremost in battle with her *"Sic semper tyrannis"* emblazoned upon her shield, stands a queen-mother, haughty, fearless, wronged, oppressed and devastated, but independent still.

Sparta, Athens, and even the Switzer's home, must give the palm to thee, thou honored mother of States and statesmen. Your sons have poured out their life blood for your honor, and your daughters are heroines.

The attitude of Virginia is the most sublime that has ever fallen to any State to enjoy. Her fields are made desolate, her houses rendered homeless, her people beggars, yet the haughty and invincible spirit of her sons and daughters still brooks no control, and invites extermination rather than submission. And the great old queen of war, with her garments all blood-stained and tattered by a hundred conflicts, surveys with calmness the desolation around, casts a tearful glance upon her fallen braves, smiles triumphantly upon the battling hosts, and in stern, defiant tones, she cries—"if I perish, I perish."

As I walked the streets of Richmond, I could but sigh at the contrast between the appearance of my own country and that of the countries I had just traveled through. There, plenty, and gaiety, and wealth, and happiness, seemed to abound; here, in my own land, in the proudest and most chivalric city in America, want and penury stalked hand in hand. The ladies of the land, pale and grief-worn, glided along, clothed in the habiliments of mourning; old men and boys, and sick and wounded soldiers, crowded the public places, whilst artillery and ammunition trains rumbled noisily along the stony ways. I asked myself if there was no vengeance on high, no righteous arm to save, no interceding voice to stay the destroyer. Yet, these people appeared to rise in spirits, as the enemy approached nearer. Whilst the thunder of Grant's cannon shook the window-panes in the capitol, and the rattling musketry was borne in fearful distinctness upon the air, the ladies might be seen quietly shopping in the stores, and the little boys in their mimic military arrays, could be heard crying aloud, "Gen. Lee is whipping Grant again to-day."

I happened to arrive in Richmond just when Grant was marshaling his mighty army on the north bank of the Rapid Ann. This was, I believe, the seventh attempt upon the rebel capitol. The great Ulysses, the hero of Vicksburg, assumed chief command, and boasted that the "rebels should find their last ditch."

It was a sublime spectacle to regard these two opposing armies. Grant remained until he had men enough. Gen. Lee, with his little army of heroes and veterans, faced him, and, in sullen tones, his cannon thundered—"thus far shalt thou come, but no farther." On the night of the 4th of May [1864] the Federals commenced crossing the river, and on the 5th our army attacked their advance and drove them back towards the Rapid Ann.

At dawn on the 6th Grant made a furious and desperate assault on our right wing, drove it in, and his masses, in the pride and confidence of temporary victory, were met by Longstreet's corps, which had just come up in time. This was the great battle of the Wilderness, the most terrible conflict of the war. All day the contest raged, and night found our army the victors. Owing to the thick undergrowth and the almost impenetrable woods, very little artillery could be used, but the musketry was appallingly severe. Some idea of the great fierceness of this fight may be gained from the fact, that an oak-tree, more than a foot in diameter, was literally cut down by bullets, and pieces of this tree may be seen upon the mantels of many a Virginia home, as relics of the mighty struggle.

After this battle, Grant commenced the famous sliding movement, which finally brought him within nine miles of Richmond.

Next, after the Wilderness fight, came the battle of Spottsylvania Court-House. Our troops had thrown up hasty rifle-pits, and against these the Federals were hurled with the fury of desperation. For more than six hours the fight raged with almost unequaled fierceness. The enemy succeeded in breaking the left of our line, and captured some three thousand prisoners and twenty guns. This, however, was the only success they met with. On all other parts of the line the infuriated and drunken vandals were repulsed with immense slaughter.

It was during this day's fearful carnage, that Grant is reported to have been sitting quietly on his horse, smoking a cigar, and aides and couriers dashed up to him for orders to their commands, receiving only one reply from the butcher of the Wilderness, viz: "send in the men." And the men were sent in, and many hundreds of Northern homes deplored this day's work.

Our army supplied themselves with blankets, clothing, shelter-tents, and every description of battle-field plunder.

After this there was a lull for some days, each army being strongly entrenched, and feints, skirmishes, &c., made up the order of every day.

In a few days, however, Grant again commenced his sliding, or, as he called it, flanking movement, and it was a race between our army and his to gain possession of the bridges, near Hanover Junction. Our army was there ahead of him, and offered battle. After some days of heavy skirmishing, he evacuated his works, and continued his flanking movement to Coal Harbor,[1] about nine miles from Richmond, and well remembered as the scene of the decisive battle between Lee and McClellan for the possession of Richmond. Our army here occupied nearly the same relative position that McClellan's did at the battle of the 27th of June, 1862. Here, again, repeated assaults were made in vain to break through our lines and capture Richmond. Grant permitted his dead and wounded to lie between the lines four or five days before he would ask a truce. However, he at last condescended to propose a flag of truce to Gen. Lee to allow both parties to bury their dead. Gen. Lee replied that he had no dead to bury, and declined the offer. Finally, Grant asked permission to bury his own dead; this was granted, and hundreds of Yankees were found with slight wounds, who had starved for food or perished for water, under the cruel and brutal policy of their commanding general.

This accords well with the notorious character of the man, and this the reward he gave those men who marched to death at his bidding.

It is true that during the whole of these operations, Grant was approaching near Richmond, but it was only by continually sliding to the left. Our army kept between him and the city always, and he was beaten in every engagement.

Finally, notwithstanding his boastful dispatch that he would "fight it out on this line, if it takes all summer," he changed his policy, crossed to the south side of the James, and tried to steal a march on Petersburg; but Beauregard was there in time and

---

[1] Often incorrectly listed as Cold Harbor; also referred to as Gaines Mill.

foiled him. Wherever he went he always found the Confederate army in his front. It has always been a mystery to me how Gen. Lee knew so much of the enemy's plans, whether he was moving as a feint or in earnest. When the history of this campaign shall become known, it will be the most astounding military feat on record, which enabled Gen. Lee to baffle such superior numbers, and gain so many victories over such odds.

Well may that great and good man take rank amongst the foremost generals of the world, and be claimed as second to none.

And he commands too the best and most devoted army that was ever gathered together.

For nearly four years the Army of Northern Virginia has been continually marching and fighting. It has fought more battles and gained more victories than any other great army of which we have any record. Its history is a proud one. And its commander, Gen. R. E. Lee, the warrior and Christian, looms up as the greatest military chieftain the world ever saw. This army yet presents its front to the foe, unconquered and unconquerable.[2] Whether on the tedious march, in the comfortless bivouac, or magnificently stemming the tide of battle, it is the same unflinching, devoted, and sacrificial host, the salvators of their country's honor. May God shield our peerless chief and the noble army of Northern Virginia.

And now, reader, the author bids you farewell. "What is writ is writ."

If you have been able to while away the *ennui* of an hour over these pages, he feels both satisfied and compensated.

[2] The memoir, published in Houston, February 5, 1865, obviously was completed by Barziza after his retirement, June 21, 1864, and before the final disastrous campaigns of the war.

BIBLIOGRAPHY

GOVERNMENT DOCUMENTS

Manuscript

Muster Rolls, 1861–1862 (Company C, Fourth Regiment, Texas Infantry, C.S.A.). Confederate Collection, National Archives, Washington, D.C.

Register, Medical Director's Office, Richmond, Virginia, undated. Confederate Collection, National Archives, Washington, D.C.

Register of the Fourth Regiment, Texas Infantry, October 19, 1864. Confederate Collection, National Archives, Washington, D.C.

Printed

Fort Fisher, State Historic Site. Issued by the State Department of Archives and History, Raleigh, North Carolina, 1962.

Official Records of the Union and Confederate Navies in the War of the Rebellion. 30 volumes. Washington, D.C.: Government Printing Office, 1894–1922.

Texas Legislature. *The House Journal of the 15th Legislature.* Galveston, Texas: Shaw and Blaylock, State Printers, 1876.

Union Army: A History of Military Affairs in the Loyal States, 1861–1865, The. 8 volumes. Washington, D. C.: Government Printing Office, 1880–1901.

War of the Rebellion: Official Records of the Union and Confederate Armies. 128 volumes. Washington, D.C.: Government Printing Office, 1880–1901.

PRIVATE PAPERS

Townsend (Captain William Purnell) Letters. Thomas Townsend, 1108 Gaston Street, Austin, Texas.

NEWSPAPERS

Austin Weekly Statesman, 1878.
Dallas Herald, The, 1858–1876.
Galveston Daily News, 1874–1882.
Houston Chronicle, 1940.
Houston Daily Post, 1882.
Houston Daily Telegraph, 1867.
Houston Tri-Weekly Telegraph, 1865.

BOOKS

Bogart, Ernest Ludlow. *Economic History of the American People.* New York: Longmans, Green and Company, 1939.

Boyd, Julian P. (ed.). *The Papers of Thomas Jefferson.* Princeton: Princeton University Press, 1950.

Burke, James (ed.). *Burke's Texas Almanac and Immigrant's Handbook for 1883.* Houston: B. F. Hardcastle and Company, 1883.

Butler, Benjamin Franklin. *Butler's Book.* Boston: Thayer, 1892.

Carroll, Benajah H. *Standard History of Texas from a Study of the Original Sources.* Knoxville, Tennessee: H. W. Crew and Company, 1912.

Clark, George. *A Glance Backward, or, Some Events in the Past History of My Life.* Houston: Press of Rein and Sons Company, 1914.

Creighton, Donald G. *A History of Canada.* Boston: Houghton Mifflin, 1958.

Davis, Nicholas A. *Campaign from Texas to Maryland, with the Battle of Sharpsburg.* Richmond, Virginia: Presbyterian Committee of Publication of the Confederate States, 1863.

Doubleday, Abner. *Gettysburg Made Plain.* New York: The Century Company, 1888.

Dunaway, W. F. *History of Pennsylvania.* New York: Prentice-Hall, 1935.

Dyer, John P. *The Gallant Hood.* Indianapolis and New York: Bobbs-Merrill, 1950.

Erath, George B. (dictated to Lucy A. Erath). *Memoirs of Major George B. Erath.* Austin: Texas State Historical Association, 1923.

Evans, General Clement A. (ed.). *Confederate Military History.* 12 volumes. Atlanta: Confederate Publishing Company, 1899.

Everett, Donald E. (ed.). *Chaplain Davis and Hood's Texas Brigade.* San Antonio: Press of Trinity University, 1962.

Gould, Hannah Flagg. *The Diosma.* Boston: Phillips, Sampson and Company, 1851.

Hicks, Irl R. *The Prisoner's Farewell to Johnson's Island, or, Valedictory Address to the Young Men's Christian Association of Johnson's Island, Ohio—A Poem.* St. Louis: Southwestern Book and Publishing Company, 1872.

History of Texas, Together with a Biographical History of the Cities of Houston and Galveston. Chicago: The Lewis Publishing Company, 1895.

Hood, John Bell. *Advance and Retreat.* New Orleans: G. T. Beauregard for the Hood Orphan Memorial Fund, 1880.

Keller, Allan. *Thunder at Harper's Ferry.* Englewood Cliffs, New Jersey: Prentice-Hall, 1958.

Kittrell, Norman G. *Governors Who Have Been and Other Public Men of Texas.* Houston: Dealy-Adey-Elgin Company, 1921.

Langer, William L. (ed.). *An Encyclopedia of World History.* Boston: Houghton Mifflin Company, 1948.

Lasswell, Mary Lubbock (ed.). *Rags and Hope: The Memoirs of Val C. Giles.* New York: Coward-McCann, 1961.

Livermore, Thomas L. *Numbers and Losses in the Civil War in America: 1861–65.* Bloomington, Indiana: Indiana University Press, 1957.

Lonn, Ella. *Foreigners in the Union Army and Navy.* Baton Rouge, Louisiana: Louisiana State University Press, 1951.

Parker, Richard Denny. (Nona Clement Parker, ed.). *Historical Recollections of Robertson County, Texas.* Salado, Texas: Anson Jones Press, 1940.

Polley, Joseph B. *Hood's Texas Brigade.* New York: The Neale Publishing Company, 1910.

————. *Soldier's Letters to Charming Nellie, A.* New York: The Neale Publishing Company, 1908.

Richardson, James D. (ed.). *Messages and Papers of the Confederacy.* 2 volumes. Nashville, Tennessee: United States Publishing Company, 1906.

Shepperson, A. B. *John Paradise and Lucy Ludwell of London and Williamsburg*. Richmond, Virginia: The Dietz Press, 1942.

Simpson, Colonel Harold B. *Gaines Mill to Appomattox: Waco & McLennan County in Hood's Texas Brigade*. Waco, Texas; The Texian Press, 1963.

Trefousse, Hans L. *Ben Butler: The South Called Him Beast!* New York: Twayne Publishers, 1957.

Tucker, Glenn. *High Tide at Gettysburg*. New York: Bobbs-Merrill, 1958.

Webb, W. P., H. B. Carroll, *et al.* (eds.). *The Handbook of Texas*. 2 volumes. Austin: Texas State Historical Association, 1952.

Williams, Kenneth P. *Lincoln Finds a General*. 5 volumes. New York: Macmillan Company, 1950.

Winks, Robin W. *Canada and the United States: The Civil War Years*. Baltimore: Johns Hopkins Press, 1960.

ARTICLES

Hogan, William Ransom. "Rampant Individualism in the Republic of Texas," *Southwestern Historical Quarterly*, XLIV, No. 4 (April, 1941), 454–480.

Shepard, Frederick J. "The Johnson's Island Plot, An Historical Narrative of the Conspiracy of the Confederates, in 1864, To Capture the U.S. Steamship Michigan on Lake Erie, and Release the Prisoners of War in Sandusky Bay," *Publications of the Buffalo Historical Society*, IX (1906), 1–51.

Shuffler, R. Henderson. "Decimus et Ultimus Barziza," *Southwestern Historical Quarterly*, LXVI, No. 4 (April, 1963), 501–512.

———. "A Texas Profile: Decimus et Ultimus Barziza," *Texas Bar Journal*, XXVI, No. 4 (April, 1963), 303–304, 344–346.

INDEX

Advance and Retreat: xi
*Adventures of a Prisoner of War,
The:* rarity of, ix; anonymity of,
ix–xi; identification of, ix, x; pub-
lication of, ix, x; description of, x;
price of, x; period covered by, 37
Allen, Col. R. T. P.: 23
Alpha, the: 117
America, colonial: 3
Antietam, Battle of: 29
Archer, Brig. Gen. J. J.: description
of, 93; imprisoned at Johnson's
Island, Ohio, 93, 99–100
Army of Northern Virginia: 125
Army of the Potomac, U.S.: 37
artillery bombardment: description of,
27–28; reaction to, 44; Texas Bri-
gade under, at Gettysburg, 44 and
n.
Ashby's Gap, skirmish of: 38, 39 n.
Asheville, N.C.: 18 n.
Athens: 121
Austin, Texas: 10 n.
Austrian military academy: 88 n.

Baltimore, Md.: and Gettysburg
wounded, 61; kindness of citizens
of, 61–63; wartime description of,
64; mentioned, 65
Baltimore Pike: 54
Bane, Capt. J. P.: 21
Barziza, Cecelia Amanda Bellett: line-
age and marriage of, 5; grave of,
16 n.–17 n.; descendants of, 18 n.
Barziza, C. R.: 18 n.
Barziza, C. Wenzel: 18 n.
Barziza, Count Antonio: 5
Barziza, Countess Lucy Paradise: 5
Barziza, Decimus et Ultimus: as so-

phisticated observer, x; articles concerning, xi, 3 n.; birth and naming
of, 6; comes to Texas, 6; receives
law degree, 7; commissioned 1st
lieutenant in Fourth Texas Infantry, 7; in Federal hospitals, 7;
reaches Texas, 7–8, 119; promoted
to captain, 7, 25 and n.; wounded
at Gettysburg, 7, 29 and n., 45,
46n.; taken prisoner, 7, 45; es-
capes prison train, 7, 105; writes
memoir, 7, 125 n.; becomes hotel
clerk, 8; reads law, 8; pleads first
murder case, 8–9; quarrels with
Col. C. C. Gillespie, 9 and n., 10,
11; eloquence of, 9, 15–16; as
active Democrat, 11; in Gov. Davis
controversy, 11–12; as chairman
of election returns committee (Jan.
1874), 11–12; in Fourteenth Texas
Legislature, 11–13; in race for
speakership, 13; in Fifteenth Texas
Legislature, 13–14; in fight on railroad subsidy, 13 and n., 14; nick-
named "Bar," 13, 20; resigns from
Legislature, 14 and n.; ends political career, 15; is touted for
Lieut. Governor, 15; and Houston
Land and Trust Co. (Houston
Bank and Trust Co.), 15 and n.;
as criminal lawyer, 15; marriage
of, 16 n.; death and funeral of, 16
and n.; grave and epitaph for, 17
and n.; eulogized, 17; portrait of,
17–18; elected 1st lieutenant of
"Robertson Five-Shooters," 19–20;
enlists in Confederate Army, 20;
arrives in Virginia with Company
C, Fourth Texas Regiment, 22;
commands company, 23; marches

through Williamsburg, Va., 24; under first fire, 24; leads attack on Yankee outposts, 24–25; commended by Hood, 25; leads Company C, 29; presentiments on invading North, 40; inactive under cannonade, 44; at Baltimore, Md., 63; thoughts of, on death, 50; enmity of, for Yankees, 72; reports to Confederate Secretary of War, 98; leaves Johnson's Island Prison, Ohio, 104; arrives Sandusky City, Ohio, 104; pawns ring for funds, 106 and n., 107; poses as Yankee veteran, 107; in New York City, 108; at Troy, N.Y., 108; enters Canada, 109; in Montreal, 110; and Canadians, 112; in Quebec, 112; in Bermuda, 117; en route to Confederacy, 117–119; returns to Virginia, 121

Barziza, Don W.: 18 n.

Barziza, Edgar Antonio: 17 n.

Barziza, Edgar Athling: 17 n.

Barziza, Edward H., Sr.: 18 n.

Barziza, E. H., Jr.: 18 n.

Barziza family: genealogy of, 3–6; family burial plot, 16; members of, in Houston, Tex., 18 n.

Barziza, Francis Louis: grave of, 17 n.; mentioned, 6 and n.

Barziza, Frank: See Barziza, Francis Louis

Barziza, G. M.: 18 n.

Barziza, H. D.: 18 n.

Barziza, James H., Sr.: as grandnephew of D. et U. Barziza, x; owns rare copy of The Adventures . . . , x; as source for editor, xii, 4 n., 15 n., 16 and n.; mentioned 18 n.

Barziza, James Lee: 17 n.

Barziza, John Paradise: 17 n.

Barziza, Lucy Ludwell (infant): 17 n.

Barziza, Patricia Nicholas (Mrs. Decimus et Ultimus): 16 and n.

Barziza, Phillip Dorsey, Sr.: as relative of D. et U. Barziza, xii, 15 and n., 16 and n.; mentioned 17 n., 18 n.

Barziza, Phillip Dorsey, Jr.: 18 n., 106 n.

Barziza, Phillip H., Sr.: 18 n.

Barziza, Phillip Henry: 4 n., 18 n.

Barziza, Phillip Ignatius, Sr.: birth of, 5; comes to America, 5; and litigation of inheritance, 5; becomes United States citizen, 5; marriage of, 5; grave, 16 n.; descendents of, 18 n.; mentioned, 106 n.

Barziza, Phillip Ignatius, Jr.: grave of, 17 n.; descendents of, 18 n.; mentioned, 6, 8 and n., 17 n.

Barziza, Phillippa Ludwell: grave of, 17 n.

Barziza, P. I.: See Barziza, Phillip Ignatius, Jr.

Barziza, Robert A.: 18 n.

Barziza, Sarah Mountcastle (Mrs. William Lee): grave of, 17 n.

Barziza, Viscount Filippo Ignacio. See Barziza, Phillip Ignatius, Sr.

Barziza, William Lee: grave of, 17 n.; mentioned, 4 n., 6, 18 n.

Barziza Street: 18 and n.

Bastrop, Felipe Henrique Neri, Baron de: 3

Bastrop Military Institute: 23

Bastrop, Texas: 23

"Battle of Gettysburg, The": 84–87

Baylor, R. E. B.: 7

Baylor University: 7

Beall, Brig. Gen. William N. R.: description of, 94; as prisoner at Johnson's Island, 94

"Beast Butler." See Butler, Maj. Gen. Benjamin F.

Beauregard, Gen. Pierre Gustave, Toutant de: at defense of Richmond, Va., 124; mentioned, 120

Belette, Cecile. See Barziza, Cecelia Amanda Bellett

Belle Isle, Va.: and Confederate prisoners, 92

Bellett, Cecelia Amanda. See Barziza, Cecelia Amanda Bellett

Bermuda: Confederate activity in, 117; mentioned, ix, 7, 117, 119 n.

blockade runners: operation of, 117–118; mentioned, 7
Block House Spring, Texas: 20
Bonner, T. R.: 13
Boonsboro, Battle of: 29
Boston, Mass.: 114
Boswell, James: 4
Botts, Col. W. B.: 15, 16 n.
Bourbon Co., Ky.: 96
Bragg, Gen. Braxton: 38 n.
Braine, John C.: 115 n.
Braunfels, Carl. *See* Solms, Prince of
Brazos River: 19 n.
British troops in Canada: attitude toward Yankees, 111, 116; attitude toward Confederacy, 111; Victoria Guard, 111; devotion of, to Queen and English constitution, 111–112; mentioned, 110–111
Brough, John, of Ohio: 101–102
Brown, John: 94 and n., 95 n.
Brown, Lt. William Morton: 62 n., 99 n.
Bruton Parish Church, Va.: 4, 17 n.
Bryan, Texas: 11
Buchanan, James: 88n., 115 n.
Buckingham Co., Va.: 16 n.
Buell, Maj. Gen. Don Carlos: 88 n.
Buford's Cavalry: 43 n.
Burgess, William S.: 96
Burgesses, House of, Va.: 4
Burke's Texas Almanac and Immigrant's Handbook, for 1883: 17
Burlington, N.Y.: 109
Burnside, Maj. Gen. Ambrose E.: at Cumberland Gap, 94; orders execution of Confederate prisoners, 96; "death order" No. 38, 95 and n., 96 n.
Burr family: 4
Butler, Maj. Gen. Benjamin F.: despised by Rebels, 89–90 and n.; visits prisons, 89–90; in New Orleans, 90 n.; General Order No. 28, 90 n.; sought as outlaw, 90 n.; mentioned, 103
Byrd family: 4
Byron, George Gordon, Baron: 119

California: 17 n.

Calvert, Texas: 19 n.
Campbell, John W.: 95 n.
Campbell, Thomas N.: 96
Camp Douglas, Ill.: 95
Camp Earl Van Dorn, Texas: 20, 21
"Camp Texas," Va.: 22
Canada: assistance of, to Confederate prisoners, ix, 78, 79 n., 80 and n.; and Yankees, 115–116; mentioned, 7, 119 n.
Canada East: 113
Cape Fear River: 119 n.
Capitol of Texas: 11
Carter, Capt. Benjamin F.: 21
Cavalry, Confederate: 39, 43 n.
Cavalry, Federal: 28
Cedar Point, Ohio: 80
Cemetery Ridge: 43 n.
Chambersburg, Pa.: 42 and n., 43, 56 n.
Chambers County, Texas: 7, 17 n.
Chancellorsville, Battle of: 37 n.
Charles City Co., Va.: 17 n.
Charleston, S.C.: 56
Charleston, Va.: 94 n.
Chenowath, B. D.: 11 n.
Chesapeake, the: 114–115 and n.
Chesapeake Affair: 114, 115 n., 116 n.
Chester, Pa.: 64–66, *passim;* mentioned, 69, 72, 73 n.
Chicago, Ill.: 79 n.
Chickahominy River: 24
Chickamauga, the: 117 n.
Chippokes plantation: 3
Choctaw Indian captain: 98
Cincinnati, Ohio: 95
City of Petersburg: 117
Civil War: Confederate and Yankee views of: 58, 59–60
Clairmount, Lord: 5 n.
Clark, Edward, Gov. of Texas: 20
Coal Harbor, Battle of: 124 and n.
Coke-Davis confrontation: 11–12
Coke, Richard: 11, 12, 14 n.
Cold Harbor. *See* Coal Harbor, Battle of
Cologne, Prussia: 10 n.
Colt's rifles: 19
Company C, Fourth Texas Infantry, Hood's Brigade, C.S.A.: organized,

19; sent to Virginia, 21; redesignated, 22; at Dumfries, 23–24; at Eltham's Landing, 24; led by Barziza, 29; at Gettysburg, 46 n.; mentioned, xi, 8 n., 45 n.

Company I, Second Kentucky Infantry, C.S.A.: 95

Company K, First Mississippi Infantry, U.S.A.: 19 n.

Confederate Congress, House of Representatives: 115 n.

Confederate Hospital, Chester, Pa.: 66

Confederate Navy: 79 n.

Confederate Point (Federal Point), N.C.: 119 n.

Confederate States: 62

Confederate yell: 45

"Copperheads": 101

Crimean War: 116 n.

Cromwell, Oliver: 71–72

Culpeper Court House, Va.: 38

Culpepper, Va.: 39 n.

Culp's Hill: 46 n.

Cumberland Gap, Tenn.: 93, 94

Cumberland Valley: 42

Curtin, Andrew Gregg: 71 n.

Cushing, E. H.: 11 n.

Dacotah, the: 115 n.

Dallas Herald, The: 6 n., 11 n.

David's Island, N.Y.: 64

Davis, Edmund J.; 11, 12

Davis, Jefferson: in Mexican War, 19 and n.; sets day of fasting and prayer, 67–68 and n.; outlaws Benjamin F. Butler, 90 n.; mentioned, 106, 115 n.

Davis, Col. J. Lucius: 94 and n.

Davis, Chap. Nicholas: 21, 22, 25 and n.

DeBray, X. B.: 11 n.

DeGress, Lt. Col. Jacob C.: 10 and n.

Democratic State Convention, Texas: 11

Dessie, Uncle. *See* Barziza, Decimus et Ultimus

Devil's Den: 46 n.

Dinwiddie, Robert: 4

Diosma, The: 51

"Dixie": 66

Doneganna Hotel: 109

Doubleday, Maj. Gen. Abner: 43 n.

dueling oath, Texas: 9 and n.

Duke's Kentucky Regiment: 96

Dumfries, Va.: 23

Eastern Lunatick Hospital: 4, 5

Edith, the: 117 and n., 118

Eltham's Landing, Battle of: 24

Emmetsburg Road, Gettysburg, Pa.: 45 n.

England: 3, 4

Episcopal Church: services of, for imprisoned Confederates, 73 and n.; and *Book of Common Prayer,* 73 n.

Ewell, Lt. Gen. Richard S.: in attack on Winchester, 39 and n.; mentioned, 38, 43 and n., 86, 93

Farragut's fleet: 90 n.

Fayette Co., Va.: 95

Fayetteville, Pa.: 43

Federal Point, N.C. *See* Confederate Point

Federal prisoners of Rebels: treatment of, 91–92

Field Hospital, Twelfth Corps: 53

Fifteenth Texas Legislature: 13, 14 and n.

Fifth Michigan Cavalry: at Snicker's Gap, 39 n.

First New Jersey Cavalry: 39 n.

Florida, the: 117

Fort Delaware: 88 and n., 89, 91

Fort Fisher, N.C.: 119 and n.

Fort Sumpter, S.C.: 58

Fourteenth Texas Legislature: 11

Fourth Texas Infantry, Hood's Texas Brigade, C.S.A.: other memoirs concerning, xi; organized, 22–23; at Eltham's Landing, 24; named "Hell Roaring Fourth," 26; at Gaines Mill, 26–28; mentioned, 7, 8 and n., 20 n., 25 n.

Franklin, Benjamin: 4

Franklin, Texas: 7

Frazer, Brig. Gen. J. W.: description of, 94; imprisoned at Johnson's

Island, 94; surrender of, to Burnside, 94
Fredericksburg, Battle of: 29
Fredericksburg, Va.: 23, 38 n., 58
Freedman's Bureau: 10 n.
Freeman's Ford, skirmish of: 29
French Empire: 72

Gaines Mill, Battle of: Barziza's account of, 26–28; mentioned, 25
Gaines Mill, Second Battle of. *See* Coal Harbor, Battle of
Galveston Daily News: 12 n.
Gettysburg, Battle of: first day, 43 and n.; Confederate line retires, 45; infantry duel in, 45, 46 n.; second day, 44–46 *passim;* troop losses, 46; third day, 53–55 *passim,* 54 n.; wounded, 54 and n.; fourth day, 56; Lee's retreat in, 56 n.; poem about, 84–87; mentioned, x, 7, 93
Gettysburg College. *See* Pennsylvania College
Gettysburg, Pa.: arrival of Texans in, 43; Federal field hospital in, 57; condition of, after Battle, 58; wounded evacuated from, 61; mentioned, 29, 40, 43 and n., 44 and n.
Gillespie, Col. C. C.: 9 and n.; 11
Glennwood Cemetery: 5 n., 16
Goliad Co., Texas: 21
Gould, Hannah Flagg: 50–51 and n.
Governor's Council, Va.: 4
Grand Commandery, Knights Templar, of Texas: 6 n.
Grand Trunk Railway: 112
Grant, Gen. Ulysses S.: at Richmond, Va., 123–124; mentioned, 122
Great Britain: 80
Great Rebellion, the: 56
Greencastle, Pa.: 42 and n.
Green Spring plantation: 3
Gregory (captain of *Edith*): 117
Guadalupe Co., Texas: 21
Guiney's Station, Va.: 56 n.

Halifax, Nova Scotia: defenses of, 116; Yankees in, 116; mentioned, 113, 114, 115 n., 116 n.
Hannibal (Barca): 72
Hanover Junction, Va.: 38 n., 124
Hardeman Rifles: 21
Harrisburg, Pa.: 73, 105 and n.
Harrisburg, Texas: 20
Harrisburg Road, Houston, Texas: 18
Harrison Co., Ky.: 96
Harris Co., Texas: 13, 14 n., 17
Harris County (Tex.) Civil Courts Bldg.: 18 and n.
Harris County (Tex.) Courthouse: 11
Hearne, C. C.: 11 n.
Henderson, J. P.: 11
Hicks, Irl R.: quoted, 82
Hill, Lt. Gen. Ambrose P.: 38 n., 43 n., 86, 93
Hill, Col. Charles W.: 99 n.
Hill, E. P.: 15, 16 n.
Hill, W. P.: 11 n.
Hoffman Battalion, U.S.A.: 78
Holcombe, James P.: 114–115 and n., 116 n.
Holt, Joseph: 88 n.
Hood, Brig. Gen. John Bell: as author, xi; as commander, Fourth Texas Regiment, 23; commendation by, 25; leads Fourth Texas Regiment at Gaines Mill, 25–26; mentioned, 86
Hood's Division: 41, 44 n.
Hood's Texas Brigade: other memoirs concerning, xi; organized, 23; pulls back to Rappahannock River on Yorktown Peninsula, 24; at Gettysburg, 44 n.; mentioned, 7
Hooker, Maj. Gen. Joseph: 37, 38 and n.
hospital, Federal field: description of, 54–55
hospital, Johnson's Island prison: 98–99
Houston, Texas: 4 n., 5 n., 7, 15, 16 n., 18 and n., 106 n.
Houston Age: 15
Houston and Texas Central Railway Co.: 9, 20

Houston Bank and Trust Company. *See* Houston Land and Trust Co.

Houston Bar, the: 16

Houston Daily Post: 7 n., 17

Houston Daily Telegraph: 9, 10 and n.

Houston Land and Trust Co.: 15 and n.

Houston Light Guards: 16 n.

Houston Tri-Weekly Telegraph: and *The Adventures* . . ., x; mentioned, 8 n., 26 n.

Hubbard, R. B.: 12

Hungarian revolution: 88 n.

Huntingdon, Pa.: 7, 106 and n.

Huntingdon Globe, The: 106

Hutcheson, J. C.: 15, 16 n.

I.O.O.F., Webb Encampment No. 13: 16

Independence, Texas: 7

Infantry, Ohio, 128th Regiment: 78

Inkerman Plateau, Battle of: 116 and n.

Italy: 3

James River: 3, 124

Jackson, Lt. Gen. Thomas J. (Stonewall): victory of, at Chancellorsville, 37 n.; death of, 38 n.; mentioned, 39, 56 and n., 120

Jefferson, Thomas: 4, 5

Jefferson Co., Va.: 95 n.

Johnson, Samuel: 4

Johnson's Island (Ohio) prison: location and description of, 75; discipline in, 77; rations in, 77; and housing of condemned, 77, 96–97; scarcity of water in, 77–78; sutler at, 78–79; number of prisoners and guards in, 79; Yankee spies in, 80; poem about, 83–84; notable prisoners in, 93–94; Barziza interviews in, 95; execution of condemned in, 96; shackles on condemned in, 97; morale of condemned in, 97; amusements at, 97; gambling in, 98; religious exercises in, 98; attitude of guards in, 99;

cemetery of, 99; disposal of the dead in, 99 n; photograph of, sold to prisoners, 100; prisoners' snowball battle at, 101; nonofficer prisoners in, 103; Federal report on prisoners of, 103; mentioned, 7, 63 n., 73, 78, 89, 104

Jones, Brig. Gen. J. R.: 94

Jones, J. W.: 16 n.

Keith, Alexander, Jr.: 116 and n.

Kentucky, Duke's Regiment, C.S.A.: 96

Kentucky, First Infantry, C.S.A.: 96

Kentucky Rifles, First, C.S.A.: 96

Key, Capt. J. C. G.: 21

Kirby, Col. (Hempstead, Texas, planter): 8

Knights of Guadalupe: 21

Knights of Honor: Harmony Lodge No. 861, 16

Knights Templar, Grand Commandery of Texas: 6 n.

Lake Erie: 75, 99

Law, Brig. Gen. E. McIver: 44 n.

Lee, Henry (Light-Horse Harry Lee): 4

Lee, Gen. Robert E.: at Gaines Mill, 26; prepares to cross Potomac, 38 and n.; reasons of, for invading Pennsylvania, 38 n.; retreat of, from Gettysburg, 56 n.; defense of Richmond by, 124, 125; as greatest soldier, 125; mentioned, 38, 46 n., 54, 56 and n., 86, 120, 122

Libby Prison: 63 n.

Likens, Col. J. B.: 15

Lincoln, Abraham: absolute power of, 67, 102; amnesty proclamation by, 91 n.; postpones executions of prisoners, 97; mentioned, 108

Little Round Top Hill: 43 n., 46 n.

Livermore, Thomas L.: 54 n.

Liverpool, England: 115 n.

London, England: 5

Longstreet, Lt. Gen. James: at Wilderness, 123; mentioned, 38 n., 46 and n., 86

Longstreet's Corps: 123
Looscan, Michael: 16 n., 17
losses: Fourth Texas Infantry: at Gaines Mill, 26–28 *passim*
Louisiana swampland: 22
Loyall, Comdr. B. P.: 79 n.
Lubbock, F. R.: 11
Ludwell, Lucy: 4 and n.
Ludwell, Philip, I: 3
Ludwell, Philip, II: 3
Ludwell, Philip, III: 3–4
Ludwell-Paradise House: 4
Lyons, Lord (Richard B. Pamell): 80 and n.

Macedonia: 4
McClellan, Maj. Gen. George B.: deprived of command, 70–71 and n.; endorses Democrat, 71; at Richmond, 124; mentioned, 25, 56
McNulty, John: 54 and n., 57
Maffit, John Newland, Jr.: 117
Maine: 111
Malakoff Towers, Battle of: 116 and n.
Mallory, Stephen R.: 79 n.
Malvern Hill, Battle of: 29
Manassas, Second Battle of: 8 n.
Mansfield, Ohio: 73
Marrs, John: 95–96
Marshall, Col. John: 26, 27
Mason, James M.: 110 n.–111 n.
Massachusetts Infantry, 2d: 106
Masterson, Judge James: 15
Meade, Maj. Gen. George G.: 62
Medical Department, U. S. Army: 55
Memphis, Tenn.: 94
Mexican War: 19 and n.
Miami, the: 115
Michigan, the: 79
Milam Co., Texas: 20
Millican, Texas: 20
Minor, Lt. R. D.: 79 n.
Mississippi: 19
Monck, Charles Stanly, Viscount: 80 and n.
money: farmers forced to accept Confederate currency, 42 n.; fluctuation of Confederate currency, 91; in North, 1863, 66 n.

Montcalm de Saint-Veran, Marquis Louis Joseph de: 112 n.
Montreal, Canada: 79 n., 109, 112
Montreal Evening Telegram: 112
Mulford, William: 90 n.
Munson, M. S.: 11 n.
Murfreesboro, Battle of: 95
"My Love and I": 83–84
"My Maryland": 41

"Name in the Sand, A": 51 n.
Napoleon I: 120
Nash, Lieutenant, Fifth Texas Reg., C.S.A.: 24–25
Negroes: as State troops, Texas, 11
Neri, Felipe Henrique. *See* Baron de Bastrop
Newark, Ohio: 100
New Brunswick: 111, 113, 114
Newcombe, James: 12
New Orleans, La.: 22, 90 and n.
News Job Office (*Galveston News*): as printing plant for *The Adventures* . . ., x
New York City: 114, 115 n.
New York Herald: 79 n.
Nicholas Co., Ky.: 96
Ninth Cavalry, U.S.A.: 10 n.
North, the: prosperity of, 1863, 65 and n.; inflation in, 1864, 66 n.
North Carolina: 117
Northern Democrats: attitude of, toward South, 69; attitude of, toward U. S. Government, 69; Rebels' advice to, 69–70; danger of, to South, 69–70; as potential aid, 71
Nova Scotia: ix, 7, 113, 115 n., 119 n.

Oath of Allegiance: 73 and n.
Oath of Obligation Not To Bear Arms: 73 and n.
Ogdensburg, Canada: 79 n.
Ohio Volunteer Infantry, 128th: 99 n.
Old Dominion: 40
Oliver, W. C.: 16 n.
Ottoman service: 88 n.
Owen, James: as publisher of *The Adventures* . . ., x
Owensville, Texas: 7, 19

Paradise, John: 4 and n.
Paradise, Lucy Ludwell: 4 and n.
Parker, Richard Denny: 25 n.
Parsons, Mr. (Editor, *Montreal Evening Telegram*): 112
Peninsula Campaign, the: 25
Pennsylvania: 38 n., 42, 71 and n.
Pennsylvania College (Gettysburg College): 57 and n.
Pennsylvania Infantry, 71st Reg., U.S.A.: 25
Pennsylvania Military College: 66 n.
Perrenot, E. A.: 15 n.
Perryville, Ky.: 88 n.
Petersburg, Va.: 124
Pettigrew, Brig. Gen. Johnston J.: 86
Philadelphia, Pa.: 73, 105, 108
Pickett, Maj. Gen. George E.: 38 n., 54 n., 85
Pierson, Lt. Col. William S.: 78, 100, report on prisoners at Johnson's Island, 103
Pierson, Mrs. William S.: 101
Pittsburgh, Pa.: 73, 94, 105
Plains of Abraham, Battle of: 112 n.
Pleasonton, Maj. Gen. Alfred: 39 n.
Podgorze, Poland: 88 n.
Point Lookout prison, Md.: barbarous treatment of Confederate prisoners at, 89, 91; diversions at, 90; mentioned, 94, 103
Polish Legions: 88 n.
Port Hudson, La.: 94
Portland, Me.: 114, 115 n.
Potomac River: 38, 39, 40, 56 and n., 89
Prince Albert: 112
Prison, Johnson's Island: description of, 76; accommodations at, 76; rations at, 77; discipline in, 77
prisoners, Confederate: amusements of, 81, 90, 97; life of, at Johnson's Island, 81, 100–101; and debating societies, 82; play-acting by, 83; poetry of, 82 n., 83; gambling by, 98; burial of, Johnson's Island, 99; numbers received, Johnson's Island, 99 n.; discharged, Johnson's Island, 103; escaped, Johnson's Is-

land, 103; exchanged, Johnson's Island, 103; executed, Johnson's Island, 103; deaths of, at Johnson's Island, 103; number of, Johnson's Island, Jan. 18, 1862-Jan. 18, 1864, 103; shot by sentinel, Johnson's Island, 103; transferred, Johnson's Island, 103
Puritanism: in North, 57–58; despotism of, 72

Quebec, Canada: description of, 112

Radical Republican party: 11–12
Rapid Ann (Rapidan) River: 122
Rappahannock River: 24, 37, 38 and n.
Rebellion, cause of: 58–59
Reciprocity Treaty: 111
Reconstruction: 11
Redan, Battle of: 116 and n.
Republican Party: 70–71
Republican State Committee, Texas: 10 n.
Richardson, Willard: as publisher of *The Adventures . . .*, x
Richmond, Va.: treatment of Federals by Rebels in, 91–92; desolation of, 122; siege of, 122–123, 124; mentioned, 22, 24, 26 n., 29, 38 n., 94, 103
Rich Neck plantation: 3
Ritchie, W. J.: 114
Riviere Du Loup: 113
Roberts, L. F.: 15 n.
Robertson Co., Texas: 6, 7, 19, 20
Robertson Five-Shooters: organized, 19; equipment abandoned by, 22. *See also* Company C, Fourth Texas Infantry, Hood's Brigade, C.S.A.
Robertson, Sterling Clack: 19 n.
Robespierre, Maximilien de: 5 n.
Rockbridge Artillery, Army of Northern Virginia, C.S.A.: 62 n.–63 n., 99 n.
Rocketts, Va.: 22
Round Top Hill: 44 n., 46 n.
Rousse's Point: 109
Royal Society of London: 4

Rusk House: 8
Rust, W. M.: 15 n.

St. Georges, Bermuda: 117
St. John, N. B.: 114
St. Lawrence River: 113
St. Louis, Mo.: 88
Saligny, Alphonse, Count de: 3
Sandusky Bay: 75
Sandusky City, Ohio: 73, 75
Sanger, D. B.: 46 n.
San Jacinto, the: 110 n.
Schoepf, Brig. Gen. Albin F.: 88 and n.
Schurz, Maj. Gen. Carl: 43 n.
secession: North's reasons for opposing, 70–71
Second Division, Eighth Army Corps, U.S.A.: 39 n.
Second Manassas, Battle of: 25 n., 29 and n.
Second Massachusetts Cavalry: 39 n.
Seddon, James A.: 79 n.
Seven Pines, Battle of: 24
Seward, William H.: 80 n.
Shenandoah Valley, Va.: 38
Sims, George P.: 96
Slidell, John: 110 n.–111 n.
Smith, Ashbel: 11
Smith Co., Texas: 13
Snicker's Gap: skirmish at, 38, 39 n.
Solms, Carl Braunfels, Prince of: 3
Sparta: 121
Spottsylvania Court-House, Battle of: 123
Steel, Capt. John: 8
Sterling, Texas: 19
Stonewall Cemetery: 18 n.
Stuart, Maj. Gen. J. E. B.: 39 n.
Suffolk, Va.: 29, 38 n.
Supreme Court, Texas: 6 n.
Switzerland: 121

Taliaferro, S.: 16 n.
Taliaferro, Brig. Gen. William B.: 94 n.
Terry's Brigade, U.S.A.: 81
Terry, Brig. Gen. H. D.: 78, 103
Texas: cosmopolitan populace of, 3;

House of Representatives of, 14 n.; admitted to Confederacy, 19; mentioned, 67
Texas and Pacific Railway Co.: 13
Texas Brigade. See Hood's Texas Brigade
Texas militiamen: 20
Texas regiments: 23
Third Missouri Infantry, U.S.A.: 10 n.
Thompson, Brig. Gen. M. Jeff.: 94
Thoroughfare Gap: skirmish at, 29
Tom Green Rifles: 21
Townsend, Capt. William Purnell: elected captain, 19 and n.; leads charge, 28; mentioned, xi, 20 and n., 21 and n., 23 and n., 26 n.
Travis Co., Texas: 21
Travis Rifles: 11
Trent Affair: 110 and n.
Trent, the: 110 and n.
Trimble, Maj. Gen. Isaac R.: 93
Trimble, Maj. Gen. J. R.: 93
Tri-Weekly Galveston News: and The Adventures . . .: x
Tucker, Glenn: 46 n.
Tucker, Nathaniel Beverly: 115 and n.
Turkey: 88 n.
Turner, E. P.: 16 n.
Twelfth Army Corps, U.S.A.: 53
Tyler, John: 115 n.

"Uncle Dessie." See Barziza, Decimus et Ultimus
Union Eleventh Corps: 43 n.
Union First Corps: 43 n.
United States: 59, 64, 80

Vallandigham, Clement L.: 101
Venice, Italy: 5, 16 n.
Vicksburg, Miss.: 56
Virginia: tidewater area, 3; Governor's Council of, 4; Barziza returns to, 121; proud and defiant, 121; mentioned, 67
Virginia, University of: 115 n.
Von Biberstein, H. R.: 15 n.

Waller Co., Texas: 8
war: horrors of, 46–47, 51; beastiality of, 49; as necessary evil, 51; and the price of liberty, 51; responsibility for, 49
Washington, D.C.: 46 n.
Washington, George: 4
Wellesley, Mass.: 18 n.
Wellington, Arthur Wellesley, Duke of: 120
Wessells, Brig. Gen. H. W.: 99 n.
West Building Hospital: 64
Wheelock, Texas: 6 and n., 7
Wigfall, Col. Louis: 23
Wild Cat Camp, Ky., Battle of: 88 n.
Wilderness, Battle of the: 123
Willard's Hotel: 88
William and Mary, College of: 6, 7, 115 n.
Williams, K. P.: 46 n.
Williamsburg, Va.: Eastern Lunatick Hospital in, 4; Restoration of, 4; mentioned, 3, 4, 5 and n., 17 n., 24, 115 n.
Williamsport, Md.: 41, 56 n.
Wilmington, N. C.: 7, 119 n.
Wilson Bldg.: 8
Winchester, Va.: 39 and n.

Winkler, E. W.: identification of *The Adventures . . .*, x
Wolfe, Maj. Gen. James: 112 and n.
Woodward, George W.: 71 and n.

Yankees: in race for Gaps, 38; appearance of women, 42; and love of flag, 42; reaction of, to Rebels, 43, 56; attitude of, toward Lee and Jackson, 56; patriotism of, 57; civilian treatment of Rebel wounded by, 57–58; described by Barziza, 58–60; ideas of, on Southerners, 60–61; hatred of South by, 60–61; as prisoners in South, 62; and kindness of ladies, 66–67; fear of, for Federal government, 67; regard of, for women, 68–69; and Oath of Allegiance, 91 and n.; treatment of Confederate prisoners by, 91–92; thought of, on Col. J. L. Davis and John Brown, 94; trickery of, 100; bitter political battles by, 101–102; subjugation of, to military, 102; resident in Halifax, Nova Scotia, 116
Yorktown Peninsula: 24
YMCA at Johnson's Island Prison: 82 n.–83 n.